Gerhard Ammerer · Harald Waitzbauer

STERNBRÄU

The history of an old-established Salzburg inn and brewery

Gerhard Ammerer · Harald Waitzbauer

STERNBRÄU

*The history of an old-established
Salzburg inn and brewery*

VERLAG ANTON PUSTET

Impressum

Sternbräu – The history of an old-established
Salzburg inn and brewery is listed in the German
national bibliography; detailed bibliographic
data can be viewed at http://dnb.d-nb.de

© 2015 Verlag Anton Pustet
5020 Salzburg, Bergstrasse 12
All rights reserved.

Cover Images: Erika Mayer
Graphic Design & Production: Tanja Kühnel
Proof-reading: Martina Schneider
English Translation: Gail Schamberger
Printed by: Druckerei Theiss, St. Stefan in Lavanttal
Printed in Austria

 6   5   4   3   2   1
20 19 18 17 16 15

ISBN 978-3-7025-0788-6

www.pustet.at

Contents

The sheer dimensions of the building site were impressive. Who can remember anything like this right in the middle of Salzburg's Old Town? The construction of the Large Festival Hall was long past, and the demolition and excavation work for the so-called "Griesgasse breakthrough" was even longer ago. Looking down from the Mönchsberg, perhaps from the terrace of the Museum of Modern Art, you could see an enormous blue crane and a huge hole amid the maze of buildings in the Old Town. You'd point down there and say: "Look, that's the construction pit for the Sternbräu!" And since seeing is not necessarily believing, people would gaze incredulously at that gaping hole and the blue crane, trying hard to visualise the familiar pre-2013 townscape.

For the majority of Salzburg residents, the Sternbräu was a permanent fixture; it had always been there, and always would be. For many people it was the scene of memories, stories, anecdotes from all seasons and occasions, from their childhood and young days, with friends, acquaintances or relatives, with a school class or colleagues, for club meetings, discussion groups or dances – or perhaps occasionally just to prop up the bar... This was the Sternbräu, an eminent and of late somewhat greying "diva" (to quote landlord Harald Kratzer). Now, suddenly, there was only this vast construction pit.

Few people are aware, however, that the building fabric of the Sternbräu had demonstrably been constantly tinkered around with for over 200 years, that the rooms on the Griesgasse side did not become the gastronomic centre of the Sternbräu until 1926, and that today's large self-service courtyard dining area ("Volksgarten") opened only in 1931, because until then the old brewery building stood in the way. But the more fast-moving the age, the more tenaciously do we cling to what is familiar.

The first stage of demolition cut many Salzburg residents to the heart.

Gaping hole and blue crane: for many months the salient features of the reconstruction.

The Sternbräu site underground –
the archaeological results of 2013/14[1]

The second town wall, completed around 1480, photo april 2013.

In the course of the Sternbräu reconstruction, part of the Late Mediaeval town wall, in an excellent state of preservation, was discovered just under ground level. After the peasant rebellion of 1462, there was a spate of construction work during the reign of Prince-Archbishop Burkhard von Weisspriach, leading to significant urban growth. Consequently, the old town wall running immediately behind the houses in the Getreidegasse was abandoned, and between 1465 and 1480 the wall-line was moved, parallel to the old one, towards the Salzach. The area thus gained had hitherto been a flood plain, so for building use it had to be filled up to a height of between one and one-and-a-half metres.

In 2013 a team of archaeologists was called in; Ulli Hampel, Birgit Niedermayr and Peter Höglinger hoped to find at least part of this wall, which had been covered up when the ground level was once again raised considerably for the third stage of fortifications at the beginning of the Thirty Years' War. To the huge surprise and delight of the archaeologists and historians, the very first probes were

The defence tower revealed during reconstruction in spring 2013 in the area between *Bürgersaal* and Sterngässchen.

successful quite close to the surface, and the wall coping was revealed. Further excavation finally exposed the wall, up to 3.9 metres high, over 1.6 metres wide at the top and more than 70 metres from east to west, running right across the large restaurant garden and on through the former Sternbräu kitchen and the *Bürgersaal*. The wall's remarkable state of preservation is due to the ground level having been raised several times up to the 18th century, to protect the site from the rising water-table and from flooding. Even while it was under construction, or shortly after-

wards, massive infilling was carried out, probably because of a flood. This brought the site by stages to the present level, so the fabric of the wall, now underground, was saved from destruction and preserved almost unaltered.

The town wall was constructed some 550 years ago as a cavity wall, with river limestones, carefully cut into ashlars, neatly placed as skins, and the cavity filled with just a little mortared rubble-stone. The gaps in the skins were mostly closed flush with mortar. The wall stands on a dry-stone base of large conglomerate blocks.

The town wall in the cellar of the Sternbräu,
as displayed after the reconstruction.

One of the authors being interviewed for the programme
"Salzburg heute" on Austrian Television in April 2014.

Particularly surprising is a horseshoe-shaped tower (walls 1.7 metres thick, interior diameter 6.8 x 5.7 metres) built on the outside of the wall in the area between the *Bürgersaal* and the Sterngässchen. It defends one of the three *Tränktore* [gateways to a watering-place for cattle] leading from the Getreidegasse through to the Salzach. In contrast to the wall, the masonry – preserved only to a height of 1.3 metres – consists of large conglomerate ashlars well-trimmed on the outer face. According to contemporary portrayals, the tower must have been added shortly after the wall was built. A central plinth probably supported a pillar bearing its upper storey. The floor level in the tower was only later raised by some 0.4 metres and a room measuring 3.3 x 1.6 metres partitioned off. The light-slits in the ground floor, shown in 16th-century vedute, proved to be embrasures (span 0.5 – 1.5 metres), which

could just be made out at the upper edge of the stub of the tower. Only on the east side was a complete window spared from more recent damage. The tower was partially demolished during construction of the houses on what is now the Griesgasse (formerly a garden established by Prince-Archbishop Paris Lodron), the stones probably being used for the foundations of the new buildings.

One of the two small latrine shafts discovered on the building site was filled with sherds – cooking vessels belonging to a household dating from around 1600 (flat-rimmed pots with handle, pan-shaped bowls, large pans, decorated plates, a yellow glazed chamber-pot, fragments of milk-bowls and many other vessels).

The date of the so-called *Sternstöckl*, a small outhouse in the north-east corner of the site, was established as being around 1600 – as indicated by green glazed wall-tiles. This structure was built directly on to the town wall, parts of which were even removed to make room for the upper storey, using the width of the fortification (1.6 metres) for extra space. In addition, a spiral staircase – of which the archaeologists managed to uncover the top three steps – was built into the ground floor in the north-west corner of the tower. In the upper storey, large areas of the Early Modern brick-tile floor had been preserved. The out-house, still in existence, was part of an originally larger building complex.

All these remarkable finds – particularly the excellent state of the exposed wall – were reason enough for the architects and their clients to make significant alterations to the building plans. At no small cost, a major part of the historic wall in the cellar of the present sales area was conserved for display to visitors.

Salzburg from the Kapuziner-berg, unknown artist and form-cutter, woodcut 1572.

The modern façade towards the open-air restaurant.

SternLounge.

The years 2013 and 2014 saw clearance, excavation, basement construction, planning, alteration, re-planning and rebuilding. Archaeologists were plying their trade amongst the building workers – and, as might have been expected, the fenced-off site became the object of curiosity and speculation. From both Getreidegasse and Griesgasse, would-be spectators tried to catch a glimpse of the construction work. To many observers, the end of the Sternbräu was apparently nigh.

When the reconstruction was complete and the result revealed – what then? The pit and the blue crane had vanished. The public flocked to get the feel of the place, with the modern façade along the courtyard area, and the windowless dining-room replaced by the new *SternLounge* – light and transparent, amply glazed.

Those wishing to satisfy their curiosity with a tour of the new Sternbräu will find features both new and familiar. Awaiting guests are the traditional *Bürgersaal*, the beer bar – now called the *Braumeisterstube* – next to the Griesgasse, and the little garden café surrounded by the arcades familiar from previous times, as well as the new *SternLounge*, *Sterngalerie* and *Sternzeit*. Architecturally, the large open-air restaurant, with self-service area in the *Sternstöckl*, is a definite improvement; so is the trattoria *La Stella* – now relocated in the former malt-house. From the completely new part of the building between the *Volksgarten* and the open-air restaurant, escalators now descend into subterranean realms – you can almost imagine gliding down to a station of the non-existent underground railway, the expediency (or otherwise) of which has been debated for decades. You are now in what is called the *Sternarkaden*, to house shops on three levels, with the idea of bringing new flagship stores into the Old Town. This expanded utilisation

Top: The traditional *Braumeisterstube*.
Next pages: *Bürgersaal* in all its new splendour.

with spacious shopping areas provides economic regeneration in that part of the Old Town which has always linked the Getreidegasse and the Griesgasse – a practical and high-quality complement to the gastronomic premises.

The escalator takes you straight down into the Late Middle Ages, or at least, to the excellently preserved remains from the period – part of the town wall and a 15th-century defence tower, both of which have been integrated into the modern structure.

Above the Late Middle Ages, you can spend the present day lazing over breakfast or sipping an aperitif in the *SternLounge*. Large windows and an elegant glass roof lend the gastronomic ambience transparency and a feeling of modern urban life. Here landlord Harald Kratzer can realise his gastronomic concept: a symbiosis of tradition and modernity, old and new, restfulness and dynamism. Kratzer looks forward to the development of an "urban mix". As ever – that is, for the past 90 years or so – Wiener schnitzel, traditional dishes and beer are served in the *Bürgersaal*, with its historical paintings by Karl Reisen-

bichler, or under the groined vault of the *Braumeisterstube*, while the *SternLounge*, *Sterngalerie* and *Sternzeit* offer the opportunity for late revellers to chill out.

In the course of the reconstruction, 13 apartments with all mod cons were constructed in the houses at Griesgasse 23 and 25. Considering all these provisions – gastronomy, accommodation, shops, ample open areas and not least the traffic-calmed Griesgasse – it may be expected that a completely new urban district, full of vitality and offering a high quality of life, will evolve around the Sternbräu.

Here we should mention briefly the features that will rarely if ever be seen by visitors to the Sternbräu. These include completely new technical installations, a new kitchen area on the Sterngässchen side, and ten 1,000-litre beer tanks to replace the traditional barrels. The house beer is the specially brewed, unfiltered "Sternbier"; the main brand is Gösser, but a variety of other specialities is also on offer. As for the cuisine, Harald Kratzer declares himself committed to "communism in its purest form", interpreted as quality affordable for all.

We could find no jubilee year to introduce the following account of the Sternbräu's history; dating back from 2014, neither century nor half-century offers memorable events with significant relation to the Sternbräu. This is not strictly necessary, however. The present authors are just as happy to invite the reader – perhaps over a glass of *Sternbier* – to a journey through time, back to the origins of the Sternbräu and its progress to the *SternLounge* of today.

Owners and restaurateur at the reopening celebration on 23 October 2014: Andreas Neumayr, Harald Kratzer, Franz Modrian and Sebastian Neumayr (from left to right).

The *Riexingerhaus* in the Trägasse
Getreidegasse, town wall and *Tränktor*

In any attempt to trace the historical development of the Sternbräu, we must first forget the present restaurant complex, since in earlier times the whole situation was completely different. From the 16th century onwards, the entrance, the premises themselves and even the address bore no resemblance to the present building. All the parts which border on the Griesgasse after the latest reconstruction and which now constitute the greater part of the large restaurant, date from the 20th century. Until then, the buildings with the current address, Griesgasse 23–25, did not exist, the main entrance having been moved to the Griesgasse only in 1926. The brewery and the restaurant belonging to it were originally housed in the buildings at Getreidegasse 34, which had in fact been three houses, but were already counted as one in the 1429 census.[2] In an early document they are mentioned as being "on the left side of the *Trägasse*, seen from the *Spitalvreythof*".[3] Since at the beginning of the 19th century the buildings were numbered away from the town centre, according to the so-called Paris system, the Sternbräu buildings are now on the right side of the Getreidegasse. Towards the Salzach, the property extended at first only as far as the newer town wall, built between 1465 and 1480 – a section of which (as mentioned in the introduction) was exposed by the archaeologists in spring 2013, during the latest reconstruction work.

What was later the Getreidegasse, in the mid-16th century. Detail from the 1553 veduta, a coloured pen drawing in the abbot's hall of St. Peter's Abbey.

Diaphragm arch in the passage at Getreidegasse 38, on the Sternbräu side.

So when were the houses on the Getreidegasse built? What did this district – the *Trägassenviertel*, as it was then called – look like in the 16th century, when the brewery is first mentioned? Salzburg's oldest merchants' quarter was in today's Waagplatz, and from there the mediaeval town grew downstream along the Salzach. Gradually, houses were built in the Judengasse, then in the Getreidegasse. Documents dating from 1104 first mention residents whose property was situated on each side of the *Trabegasse*. So the first section of the street already existed at the beginning of the 12th century, and is thus one of the oldest residential areas of mediaeval Salzburg. Soon after this, around the mid-century, three districts had taken shape: the merchants' quarter in the Waagplatz and the Juden-

gasse, the right-hand quarter on the opposite side of the Salzach, and the bridge with the Getreidegasse. Building work progressed rapidly, and around 1180/1185, at the lower end of the Getreidegasse, directly before the *Westertor* [a town gate], the *Admonter Hof* was built, along with a St. Blasius chapel, which later became the Bürgerspitals-kirche [burghers' hospital church].[4]

The first town wall was probably completed about a century later, extending from the Inner Nonntaltor to the above-mentioned *Westertor*, now the Gstättentor, and along the Getreidegasse, just behind the houses.[5] The area between the wall and the river bank was used for gardens and fields.[6] During the Late Middle Ages, the three *Tränk-tore* – the *Rathaustor*, the *upper* and *lower Tränktor* –

allowed cattle through to the river from the Getreidegasse. The *upper Tränktor* was near the Hagenauerplatz, the *lower Tränktor* around the present Getreidegasse 34–36, and thus in the Sternbräu grounds. The gate of the first fortification is still preserved as a diaphragm arch in the passage at Getreidegasse 38.

Some 200 years later, around 1480, the completion of the second town wall moved the *Tränktor* nearer to the river. Here, and at the other gates between Salzach and Getreidegasse, imposing gate-towers were erected; they were guarded, and retained their function for a long time.

The narrow – generally only two window-widths – mediaeval buildings along the Getreidegasse extended to the rear as far as the old town wall, so were not of such modest dimensions as might appear from the street. Initially, beside each house was a narrow strip of ground leading to a backyard with a garden or outbuildings. Until the devastating fire of 1270, which destroyed most of the houses, buildings were mainly of wood; rebuilding was carried out predominantly in stone. Many of the passageways and courtyards that characterise the Getreidegasse streetscape date from the ensuing period, when extensive building and reconstruction took place. The individual storeys of the new rear-ward houses had separate access stairways. This meant that not only could they be used by different households, but that, from the late 15th century onwards, condominium ownership was established – a curiosity in ownership law still partially extant as a relict of that age.[7]

The new access arrangement of the houses, around 1400, brought about a major alteration in the street façade. The individual buildings along the Getreidegasse were increasingly linked by fire-walls and thus joined into groups.

Sources name the first known owner of the house at Getreidegasse 34 – which at the time had no street name or number – in 1415 as a shoemaker called Hanns Hauswirt. In 1432, an unnamed blacksmith lived and worked there, and in 1467 one Hanns Hausner. In 1474, a *Peter Smid by the Tränktor and the clerk* is mentioned.[8]

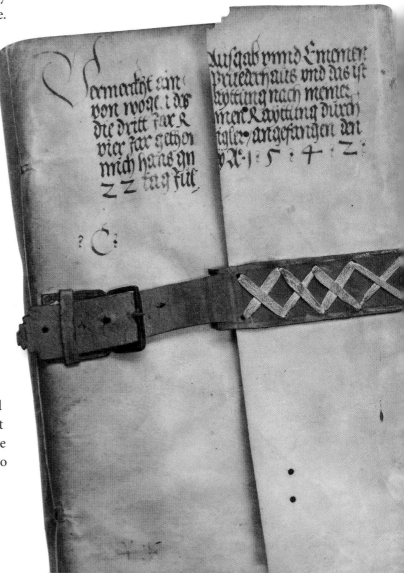

The first mention of the brewery: 1543

Record of a disbursal and purchase for the Paumgartner Endowment, as follows:

Likewise, I, Hanns Bürgler, currently trustee of the Paumgartner Endowment, have purchased, with the knowledge and permission of the respected municipal council from Hanns Riexinger, citizen of Salzburg, and his wife Kunigunde, on payment of the stated sum of 10 Pfund Pfennige [pound pennies] property tax in Salzburg currency, a plot on which stands a house in burgage and a stabling here in the town of Salzburg in the Getreidegasse, between the house of Lienhart Puchler and that of the farrier Wolfgang Schwingenhaimer, in the condition that they (= the vendors) occupied it, together with the stabling and the brew-house behind and all appurtenances without exception, in accordance with the relevant bill of sale drawn up by the honourable and established Georg Schrettl zu Kölnperg, currently municipal judge in Salzburg, dated Shrove Sunday of the 43rd year (4 February 1543), for which I paid 200 gulden on behalf of the Paumgartner Endowment.

I herewith present my claim under my expenditure in the annual accounts, etc.

On each Candlemas-Day (2 February) of Our Lady the above-mentioned Hans Riexinger or his descendants shall in future render from the said half-premises of the Paumgartner Endowment the above-mentioned sum of 10 Pfund Pfennige and accordingly the first interest date on which this property tax should be rendered would then be Candlemas of the year 1544.

Bruderhaus account book 756, purchase of half a house through the *Paumgartner Endowment*, 4 February 1543.

Like that of all the Salzburg breweries established during the 15th and 16th centuries, the founding date of the Sternbrauerei (later thus named) is not known. A first mention is to be found in a bill of sale concerning half-ownership of the property *in the Tragasse situated between Liennhart Puchler's and Wolffganng Schwingenhaimer*[9] *the blacksmith's houses* – today Getreidegasse 34. The brewery, together with the adjoining stall and all fittings and fixtures, is sold by Hanns Riexinger, the first brewer mentioned, and his wife Frau Kunigunde to the so-called Paumgartner Endowment. Its trustee, Hanns Bürgler, obtained the permission of the town council and in the name of the foundation purchased *half the premises … together with the stabling and brew-house behind* for the sum of 200 gulden.[10] The contract was drawn up by the municipal judge on 4 February 1543, but is to be found in the Bruderhaus [friary] account book dated 1542. This

year is also the first mention – in Franz Valentin Zillner's history of the town of Salzburg (1885) – of Riexinger as a brewer.[11] It is certainly probable that the purchase was finalised then, but that the actual contract was not signed until February 1543. The property is entered in the land charge register: *One Hanns Riexinger owns a house and garden in the Trägasse, next door to Hanns Lebrer his house, aforetime two half houses.*[12]

Over the ensuing years, the name appears repeatedly in the sources, though with considerable variations in spelling (Rietzinger, Riegsinger, Runtzinger, Runsinger, etc). No personal details are known about the first brewer; it is not certain whether the mayor of Salzburg named in 1511 as Hanns Riexinger[13] was identical with the brewer, or whether they simply shared the name.

The Paumgartner Endowment, which purchased from him the part of the property with the brewery, was a very important charitable foundation for the St. Sebastian Bruderhaus, enabling over centuries provision to be made for the deserving poor, particularly alms-folk. This endowment fund instituted by Ludwig Paumgartner consisted of the donation of a house on the market square, sold in 1541 for 1300 gulden;[14] the capital was invested. The following year, the Endowment purchased properties including the brewery half of the Getreidegasse house, and leased it to the seller Hanns Riexinger, who was evidently in need of money. He continued to run the brewery as it stood, for which, according to a contract dated 1544, he had to pay the sum of 10 Pfund Pfennig [pound pennies] annually at Candlemas (2 February). This sum is noted in the Bruderhaus account books in the following years.

This makes the brewery, according to sources, the second oldest in the Getreidegasse. The Mödlhammerbräu (Getreidegasse 26) was first mentioned in 1414, the Stockhamerbräu (Getreidegasse 35) not until 1569, 26 years after the Sternbräu.[15]

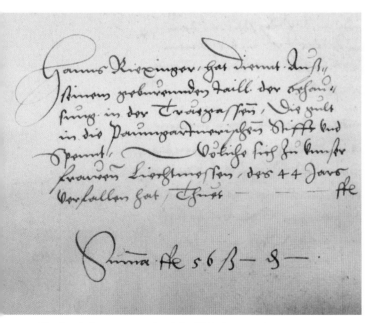

The Bruderhaus account book for 1544. As agreed by contract, Hanns Riexinger paid the sum of 10 schillings on 2 February 1544.

The brewery business probably had modest beginnings. Earliest sources mention no brewery tavern, although there very probably was one. But there is a first mention in the 1569 tax register (at which time Hans Riexinger's son Marx had been running the business for five years), listing the persons resident in the household: besides the proprietor and his wife, there were the two daughters, a labourer, two servants and – a *Kellnermaidl* [serving-maid].[16] This confirms the existence of a tavern at least since that date, but no specific name of a tavern is to be found before the

Bürgerspital account, 1571, with entry *Hans Riezinger. In the Trägasse* (line 7).

List of residents in the visitation records of 1569.

mid-17th century. Until some point in the 18th century, sources repeatedly call the property the *Riexingerhaus*,[17] which probably referred also to the brewery tavern.

In the visitation records for the year 1569, ten further persons were listed as living in four apartments in the house.[18] In the meantime, however, there had been an important change in ownership: after Hanns Riexinger's death in 1557, the son's legal guardians had bought the property back from the Bruderhaus.[19] The brewer, landlord and house-owner Marx Riexinger was followed by his son (named Hanns after his grandfather). He appears in the 1571 accounts book of the Bürgerspital [burghers' hospital] as having paid 3 gulden interest on the house.[20] Shortly afterwards, however, he sold the property to Jörg

Prau(n)seisen, who went bankrupt, and in 1581 it was purchased for Christoph Seltzeman's children Sebastian and Maria.[21]

Then in rapid succession the house was bought by Maria Sollinger (1595), Sebastian Seltzeman (1605) and a year later by Christoph Erlacher,[22] whose widow took over the business after his death in 1619.[23] Sources give no further details about these owners, nor are they particularly informative about what the brewery and tavern looked like in the era of the Riexingers and their successors. This is also the case with the other Salzburg breweries in this early period. We know from tax registers that the house had a garden.

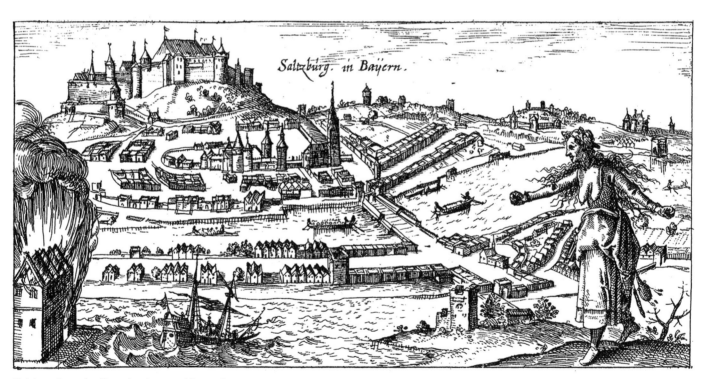

Salzburg from the Kapuzinerberg, etching and copper engraving combined, Eberhard Kieser 1623, from: *Thesaurvs philo-politicvs. Hoc est: emblemata sive moralia politica … Politisches Schatzkästlein guter Herren vnd bestendiger Freundt. Das ist: Außerlesene schöne Emblemata vnd Moralia … in diese StammBuchs Form … gantz neu an Tag geben … Sampt gewissen Abbildungen der fürnembsten … Stätten,* Frankfurt am Main 1623.

Beer-brewing and beer-drinking in Salzburg

We can, however, establish a rough order in the history of beer-brewing and drinking in Salzburg. Let us go back a little: in the Middle Ages, before brewing was established as a profit-making trade, beer was initially brewed privately, also in Salzburg. Every householder had the right to brew beer, and this was done very simply and without great attention to purity. The grain used was rye, oats, barley or wheat. Around the mid-13th century, a master brewer named Tagno is first mentioned as a witness in a transfer agreement.[24] But just as little is known about him as about others – Gotescalh, Engelbertus, Wernher and *henricus priumeister* – mentioned in documents shortly afterwards.[25] In the late 14th century we learn a little more. The first civic breweries of which we know the locations in the town of Salzburg were established at a time when the citizens were increasingly engaged in a struggle for political participation in municipal government,[26] and trade and mining were flourishing. The first more specific written evidence of the existence of a brewery in the town dates back to 1374. The *pierprewin hofstatt*,[27] the house belonging to a female brewer, had as yet no name; it was at today's Dreifaltigkeitsgasse 3 (later *Schlammbräu*), on the right-hand side of the river. Here the ever-popular beverage was brewed for the next 497 years.

Up to 1492, five further breweries of which we know the names and locations opened in the town; but these are known only through first mentions in the sources, while their opening dates are obscure. They were the later Gablerbräu, Mödlhammerbräu, Höllbräu, Guglbräu and Stieglbrauerei, all of which lasted at least 400 years.

During the 16th century, six breweries were established, with similar longevity: Kasererbräu (1501) was followed by Steinbräu (1528), Sternbrauerei (later so named, 1543), Stockhamerbräu and Moserbräu (1569) and finally Ber-

Beer-brewing, engraving by Johann Christoph Thiene, 1694.

gerbräu (1595). In the 17th century, the twelve civic breweries were joined by the monastery brewery of the Augustinian Hermits in the suburb of Mülln (1621) and the state-run Kaltenbräuhaus in the Kaiviertel, which functioned only temporarily as a brewery. Thus the Sternbrauerei was part of the second wave of breweries established in the town of Salzburg.

Regulation of the right to serve alcohol and introduction of alcohol tax

Even before this second phase of brewery openings, brewing and serving alcohol had already been increasingly regulated, and the citizens' original freedom greatly restricted.

There are early normative references to the consumption of beer in Salzburg inns in the first Salzburg Statute, the essential elements of which were drawn up in 1368. Here closing-time, for instance, was set, applying equally to landlords and patrons: the bell rung to signal "time" was named after what was evidently already the popular beverage – it was the "beer bell". After it had sounded, people were allowed on the streets of the town only if they made their presence known by singing or carried a lantern.[28]

Some 100 years later, in 1460, a tariff was imposed for Salzburg, laying down a maximum price for numerous products, including beer. A "quarter of beer" (the equivalent of 1.57 litres) must not cost more than 2 *pfennig*.[29] The beverage brewed in the town was considerably cheaper for consumers than wine, which was imported. After the regulations in the "Cristan Reutter'sches Stadtbuch" [statute

Ordinance for brewers of mead and beer, from the town and police ordinance decreed in 1524 by Prince-Archbishop Matthäus Lang von Wellenburg, p 1.

Salztburg, unsigned copper engraving coloured by Marcus Setznagel, Cologne, around 1575, from: *Civitates orbis terrarum* by Georg Braun and Franz Hogenberg.

book] dating from the latter half of the 15th century had laid down more precise guidelines for the right to serve beer,[30] the town and police ordinance decreed by Prince-Archbishop Matthäus Lang von Wellenburg (1519–1540) in 1524 extended the regulations for the brewing industry.[31]

For instance, the brewers, whose premises all included sties, were instructed henceforth not to allow their pigs to run free in the town, nor to feed them from troughs in front of their houses. For the last time before the catering trade was professionalised, the regulations on serving wine confirmed the general right to serve alcohol: "Every citizen shall be permitted to offer liquor for public sale, whether it be wine, mead or beer". Landlords were, however, directed to provide "the common townspeople and foreigners with fine liquor of every kind at all times",[32] and not to charge more than the specified prices. There was a distinction between the "common" or occasional host and the "public" or professional landlord, as well as between the categories of innkeeper and tavern-keeper.[33] The police ordinance, however, refers to the incipient merging of the catering categories which were strictly separated in the Middle Ages. Thus tavern-keepers were now permitted to offer accommodation, and hosts originally responsible for putting up travellers for the night could now provide food and drink. The seemingly widespread practice of diluting beer with water was strictly forbidden![34]

In the course of the 16th century there followed numerous restrictive measures, some of which were repeatedly renewed and or tightened. In the bar-rooms, patrons were exhorted to refrain from "unseemly clamour" and "the utterance of profanities".[35] In 1564, playing and singing of "bawdy songs" was prohibited, and in 1588 landlords were instructed "to prevent hubbub, quarrelling and discontent by day and night".[36] In addition, anyone staying overnight was required to register: "Every landlord serving beer, mead or wine shall be obliged every night to deliver to the town's governor a written account of each and every arrival, man or woman."[37]

A new ordinance for the catering industry came into force under Prince-Archbishop Wolf Dietrich von Raitenau (r. 1587–1611/12), who had all public-houses in his diocese inspected to ascertain their revenues. After obtaining the results, on 1 June 1595 he issued an edict concerning the serving of wine, beer and mead,[38] with several aims. Its primary purpose was to abolish the many "unofficial" taverns which not only paid no taxes, but were also alleged to proffer beverages of inferior quality. At the behest of the Archbishop, the premises permitted to remain – 35 taverns serving wine, 3 sweet wine, 5 mead, as well as 13 breweries – were granted licences tied to the premises,[39] while all other landlords had to close down.[40]

Wolf Dietrich, whose reign saw the introduction in Salzburg of the modern tax state, was extremely resourceful when it came to filling the state coffers. Amongst other measures, on 16 November 1587 he issued a mandate imposing a beverage levy, an alcohol tax on wine and spirits.[41]

In 1617, his nephew and successor, Prince-Archbishop Marcus Sitticus, had in his turn to take strict measures to deal with serious cases of negligence in the catering industry.[42]

Shortly afterwards, the Holy Roman Empire was severely shaken by the events of the Thirty Years' War. Salzburg, too, although not directly involved in the war, was nevertheless seriously affected by the mid- and long-term economic consequences. In 1620 the landlords declared to the town council that, due to current events, wine had become so expensive to buy in, that "for the benefit of the general public" they would henceforth stock and sell primarily beer.[43]

Wolf Dietrich von Raitenau in imagined pontifical regalia with allegories of Faith and Hope, oil on canvas, by Caspar Diefstetter, 1612.

General-Mandat betr. Missbrauch und Unordnungen in Wirtshäusern

Wir Marx Sittich / von Gottes Genaden / Ertzbischoue zu Saltzburg / Legat deß Stuels zu Rom / etc. Thuen hiemit khundt vnd zuwissen: Nachdem wir die zeit Vnserer Ertzbischofflichen Regierung nit ohne sonders Missfallen wahrgenommen / auch von andern glaubwürdig berichtet worden / was massen allenthalben in vnserm Lande / vil schädlicher Mißbräuch vnd Vnordnungen / beuorauß mit täglichem vbermässigen Pancketiern / Schlemmen / Prassen / sowol in denen offentlichen Wirths= als Priuathäusern / haltung allzustattlicher Hochtzeiten / Tagwerchen / auch Kindl : Maister : Todten vnd andern dergleichen vnnutzen Malzeiten vnd Fressereyen / Wie nicht weniger mit vberschwencklichem Pracht in köstlichen vnd deß gemainen Burger vnd Bawersmans Standt vngemässenen Klaidungen / etwas häuffig eingerissen vnd oberhandgenommen / dardurch nicht allein die edle Gaben Gottes schändtlicher weiß verschwendet / vnd alle Sachen in fast vnerschwingkliche staigerung gebracht / vil der Vnderthanen sambt ihren Weib vnd vnschuldigen Kindern ins Verderben und Elend gesetzt / auch nit wenig in Gefahr ihrer Seelen Seligkeit eingelaitet: Sonder vnd zuforderst die Göttliche Majestät höchlich offendirt und belaidiget / zu deme auch andere ehrliche Leuth / so mit dergleichen leichtsinnigen vnd verschwenderischen Personen / auff Trawen vnd Glauben handlen / vnd ihnen das jrige trewhertzig vnd wolmainend darleyhen / in verderblichen Schaden und Nacht(ei)l eingeführt / vnnd vmb das ihrige bößlich betrogen werden ... Als vnd hierauff empfehlen Wir hiemit in krafft dises offnen Mandats / allen vnd jeden Vnsern nachgesetzten Obrigkeiten / ernstlich vnd wöllen / daß ihr vnd ewer jeder insonderheit / ewern habenden Ambtsbestallungen vnnd darauff gelaisten Pflichten gemäß / auff die jenige Personen / welche Tag vnd Nacht im Lueder ligen / dem Müssiggang / Fressen vnd Sauffen außwarten / dagegen jr Haußwesen verabsaumen / jrer Arbeit nit pflegen noch außwarten / vnd durch sollich liederliches Leben jre Weib vnd Kinder / zu mercklicher Beschwer anderer ehrlicher Leut / an den Bettelstab fürsetzlich muthwilliger weiß bringen / ewer wachtbares Aug vnd fleissige Obacht habet / jenen dergleichen kaines wegs gestattet / sonder mit allem ernst vnd durch gebürende Gerichtsmittel dauon ab: vnd zur Arbeit vnd jrem Haußwesen anhaltet / Do aber bey ainem oder dem andern ein solches nit ersprießlich sein wollte oder würde / die Beschaffenheit Vnserm Statthalter vnd Räthen vmbständiglich berichtet / damit gegen dergleichen verwegnen haillosen Gesellen der nothwendige Ernst gebraucht / vnd andern zum Exempel / mit Verweisung deß Landts / weiln sie demselben ohne das mehr schädlich als nutz / oder in ander Weg / vnnachläßlich gestrafft werden mögen. Vnd dieweiln solchen liederlichen Leuthen / zu ihrem vnzimblichen Wesen vnd Leben / hoch vnd vil / durch das aigennützige Porgen der Wirth vnd Taferner Anlaß gegeben würdet / in deme sie sich / so sie mit paar Geld nit gefast / darauff verlassen / vnd ohne ainigen Bedacht jres Haußwesens / Weib vnd Kinder in Sauß hinein leben: Als ordnen vnd wöllen Wir / daß kein Wirth / Taferner oder Weinhandler / dergleichen verschwenderischen Personen vber fünff Gulden nit beyten noch porgen solle / Do sie aber hierüber ein mehrers ihnen anuertrawen / vnd dieselben hinnach in Abfall ihres Vermögens gerathen würden / solle jnen durch die nachgesetzte Obrigkeiten / fürdergleichen jre Anforderungen / do sie auch gar Pfandtverschreibungen darumb haben würden / ein mehrers nit als fünff Gulden erkent vnd passiert werden. Derohalben sie sich darnach zurichten vnd vor Schaden zuuerhueten werden wissen.

... Geben vnd mit Vnserm fürgetruckten Secret verfertigt / in Vnser Statt Salzburg / den 12. Aprilis, Anno 1617.

Salzburger Landesarchiv, Geheimes Archiv XXXV, Generale 1589–1644.

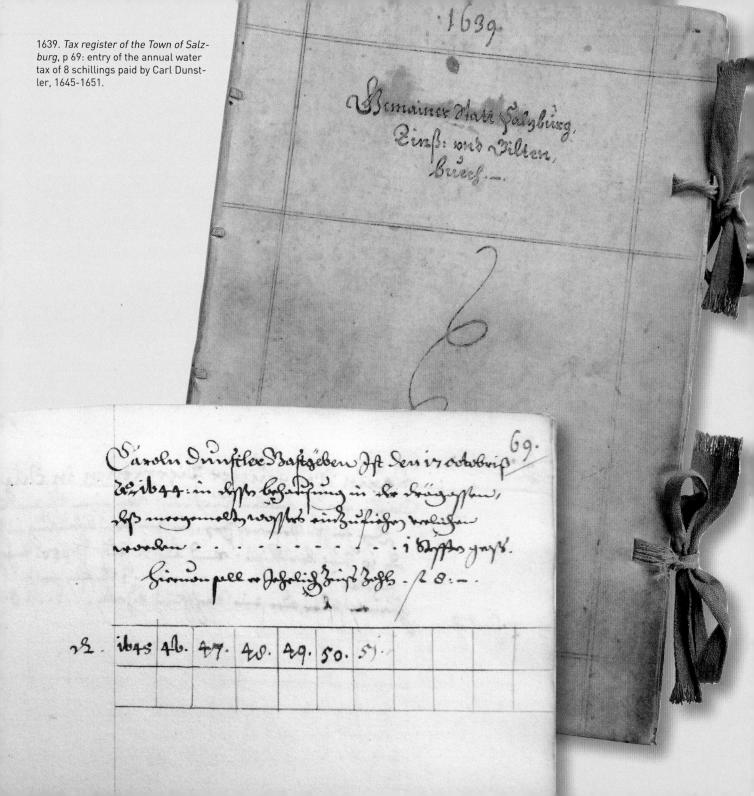

1639. *Tax register of the Town of Salzburg*, p 69: entry of the annual water tax of 8 schillings paid by Carl Dunstler, 1645-1651.

The fortifications along the River Salzach and the eponymous "Stern" bastion

The Thirty Years' War put great strain on the entire population of Salzburg, not least on the tradesmen. In a general mandate issued on 13 August 1620 – only the second year of his reign – Archbishop Paris Lodron (r. 1619–1653) extended the alcohol tax introduced by Wolf Dietrich von Raitenau to include beer.[1] Thus brewers and landlords were also obliged to contribute to the considerable expenditure necessary for armaments and construction work on the fortress. The period fixed for payment of this beverage levy (imposed initially for three years) was extended, and the tax was finally made permanent.[2] Years later, in a decree of 18 February 1636, the Prince-Archbishop imposed an additional surcharge of 8 kreutzer per bucket (= 56 ½ litres)[3] of beer, once again justifying the measure thus: *in view of the present protracted, onerous warfare, and quasi total disruption of each and every trade and commerce, in particular the almost complete failure of the salt retail, our revenues having diminished so much, and looking to diminish even further as time goes on, so that we have just sufficient for the minimum and restricted maintenance of our court.*[4]

The tax state of the Early Modern Age had evolved to the full. Prince-Archbishop Wolf Dietrich had already imposed a direct levy, the "general property tax".[5] In the tax register for 1632, the property tax for the *kleines Dunstlerhaus* – premises owned by Carl Dunstler since the early 1620s – was calculated at 3,000 gulden.[6]

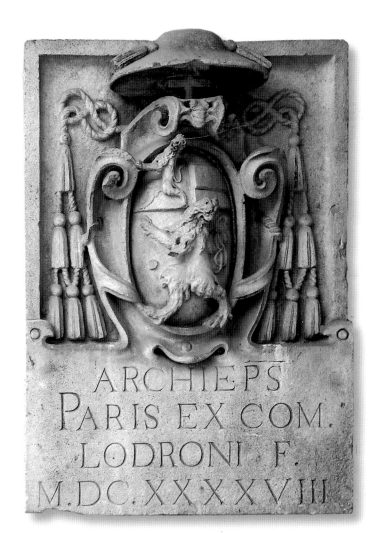

Stone relief on the last existing section of the bastions (*Zwerglgarten*, by the Mirabell Palace), showing the coat of arms of Prince-Archbishop Paris Lodron and the year 1648.

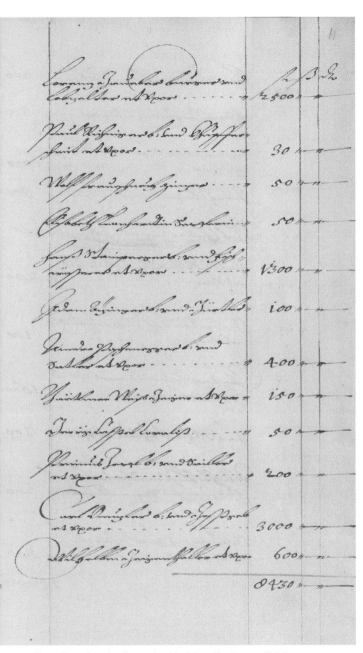

Neue Steurbeschreibung der Hochfrst. Haubtstatt Salzburg de Anno 1632, p 11, penultimate entry: tax notice for the property of the brewer and landlord *Carl Dunzler* and his wife: 3,000 gulden.

The fortifications built by court architect Santino Solari at the behest of Prince-Archbishop Paris Lodron, to ward off the military threat, were intended to make the town impregnable by extending the walls on the right bank of the river beyond the Mirabell Palace and incorporating the Fortress and the town's hills.[7]

The inn with brewery finally took its name from the nearby "Stern" bastion (clearly distinguishable in views of the town) built beside the Salzach. No precise date has been established for the naming of the entire complex. In the town's tax register (*Gemainer Statt Salzburg Zins und Giltenbuech*) of 1639 – during the Thirty Years' War – the inn was already designated as *Würthsbehausung bei dem gulden stern in der Trägassen* [hostelry at the sign of the golden star in the Trägasse].[8] It is first mentioned in the shortened form of Sternbräu in the town's land register for 1650.[9]

The "Stern" bastion, detail from a letter of patronage printed by Franz Xaver Oberer and used in 1810.

Salzburg from the Kapuzinerberg, engraving by Johann Friedrich Probst, 1700.

As shown in views from the Kapuzinerberg up to the late 16th century, development of the Getreidegasse properties to the rear had previously extended only as far as, though not beyond, the more recent town wall. Sources also mention a large tree plantation on the strip of land in front of the new *Tränktor* in the second fortifications, in the area between the repository (Getreidegasse 18–22) and the tower by the Sterngässchen (Getreidegasse 46/48).[10] When the public fountain was moved from the fish market (Hagenauerplatz) to the *Tränktor* in the Sternbräu grounds in 1599, building had just, for the first time, been carried out in front of the Gothic wall in the northern part of the property, behind the longitudinally situated "Stern" pavilion (now the entrance area to the Sternbräu from the Griesgasse).

As the ground level was raised and building carried out, the 15th-century town wall, rendered useless by the new bastions, was gradually buried. The so-called Red Tower by the *Tränktor*, now integrated into the Sternbräu grounds, was also relieved of its function by the new fortifications. On 22 December 1638, in reply to his petition, Carl Dunstler received permission from the town council to break through the now redundant town wall to insert two large windows. He had to pay a non-recurring fee of 50 gulden and a lien of 15 kreutzer annually on St. Rupert's Day (24 September).

Dunstler and his wife Ursula Gerner had owned the "hostelry at the sign of the golden star" since at least 1623,[11] and first combined the two houses at Getreidegasse 34 and 36, which appear in the land register as owned by a smith and a shoemaker.[12] After Carl Dunstler's death, the property remained in the family. The 1647 tax register lists his widow Ursula, who occupied the house together with her two sons and five daughters.[13]

Land register of the Town of Salzburg, 1650, entry concerning the handover on 7 June 1647 and the dues paid for the *hostelry, stabling and brewery in the Trägasse*. Annual dues were to: St. Peter's Abbey 2 gulden, Bürgerspital 3 gulden, Allerchristgläubige Seelenbruderschaft 2 gulden, Baron von Lamberg 4 denars

The landlord of the inn and his family had managed to pull the business through the hard times of the Thirty Years' War, shortly before the end of which the son Philipp took it over by transfer agreement on 7 June 1647. He continued to run it for a time, but 18 years later, on 7 January 1665, he sold his "lawfully inherited dwelling and smallholding" to Stefan Stockhamer,[14] owner of the *Stockhamerbräu* diagonally opposite, at Getreidegasse 35.[15]

If we look beyond the walls of the capital town of the Province at the entire area of the archbishopric of Salzburg, in the mid-17th century there were altogether 95 breweries producing almost 30,000 hectolitres of beer. The court brewery of Kaltenhausen alone, on its way to becoming the "state brewery",[16] produced a proud total of 8,000 hectolitres.[17] From the mid-17th century, after the introduction of alcohol tax on beer, all of these breweries were subjected to further huge changes and restrictions – particularly through the monopolisation in 1645 of the state brewing industry. After various intermediate stages, the "beer restriction" was introduced in 1664, under Archbishop Guidobald Thun (r. 1654–1668). From then on, the town brewers were permitted to serve their beer only in their own hostelries, but not by street sale.

Fresh water at last – the first in-house water pipeline

Archbishop Paris Lodron's financial investment in armaments and fortifications proved worthwhile. In addition to his wise policy of neutrality, this was decisive in assuring that Salzburg was not drawn into the current warfare. Although the defence measures emptied the town's coffers and made it necessary to incur debts, the everyday life of court and citizenry was not disrupted. Not only was the university – already initiated by Archbishop Marcus Sitticus – successfully founded, but new infrastructural measures were introduced. Free public wells having hitherto provided water for all the town's households, now, at the beginning of the 17th century, the demand for domestic and commercial water connections showed a marked increase.[18] During the 1630s, Salzburg's municipal authorities began to lay underground pipes in return for a fee and reimbursement of costs. Little by little, at the request of proprietors, buildings in the Getreidegasse were connected to the supply, which provided them with fresh spring water through the pipes. At first, applicants were primarily businesses, and only a few private households, which were given domestic wells. These were usually in the entrance area of the buildings, always at ground level, since the water-pressure was too low to allow a higher position.[19] The tax register, begun in 1639, listed under the heading *Water dues* those houses (and their taxes), *which drew fresh well-water pumped from the well-house by the Spital gate up through the Trägasse in an underground pipe.*[20] The water rights were initially allotted on payment of a single, relatively high fee, but on 16 June 1641 the municipal authority decided to buy back the rights already sold. Annual water dues were now charged for the already existing water-pipes and those to be laid by the well-driller, in addition to the not inconsiderable costs for laying the pipes. After the purchase price of the water

rights had been refunded, while the nearby inn *Zum goldenen Löwen*, which belonged to the *Mödlhammerbräu*, paid this fee in 1642, the innkeeper Carl Dunstler did not do so until 1645, since it was not until relatively late, on 17 October 1644 – here the tax register even gives the exact date of the installation – that the brewer and landlord had his inn connected to the water supply.[21]

Family-owned over generations: the Stockhamers

Stefan Stockhamer, the new proprietor of the *Goldener Stern*, died in 1665, only two years after purchasing it, but for several generations, until 1743, both brewery and inn remained in the family, who also owned the *Stockhamerbräu* opposite. Since Stefan Stockhamer had died intestate, all eleven children born of his first and second marriages – several of whom had married – were entitled to inherit

Wrought-iron wall bracket on the *Stockhamerbräu* with the brewers' guild sign.

equally. The Sternbrauerei was taken over by Georg Ehrenreich Stockhamer, who bought out his siblings.

His son Joseph Stockhamer succeeded him, and now, for the first time, the beer production during this period can be fairly accurately estimated. The key data are recorded in the 1700 list of beverage levies: the previous year 24 brews had been made, an average of two per month. That added up to a year's production of 336 buckets or 211 hectolitres,[22] incurring alcohol tax amounting to 181 gulden 30 kreutzer. This put Stockhamer in sixth place, ranking slightly above average, amongst the Salzburg brewers. In one respect, however, he was in a leading position, since the inspection of the copper brewing-pans, ordered that same year by the Court Chamber, showed that the *Stern Brewery*, with a capacity of 15 hectolitres per brew, had the largest brewing capacity of all the town's breweries, followed at some distance by the *Freihammerbräu* (later *Schlammbräu*) on the right-hand side of the river, with 12.5 hectolitres.[23]

What *Joseph Stockhamer brewed at the Stern*: calculation of the beverage levy for the brewing year 1700.

Protocol of the inspection of the brewing-pans in the town of Salzburg in 1700, no. 6.

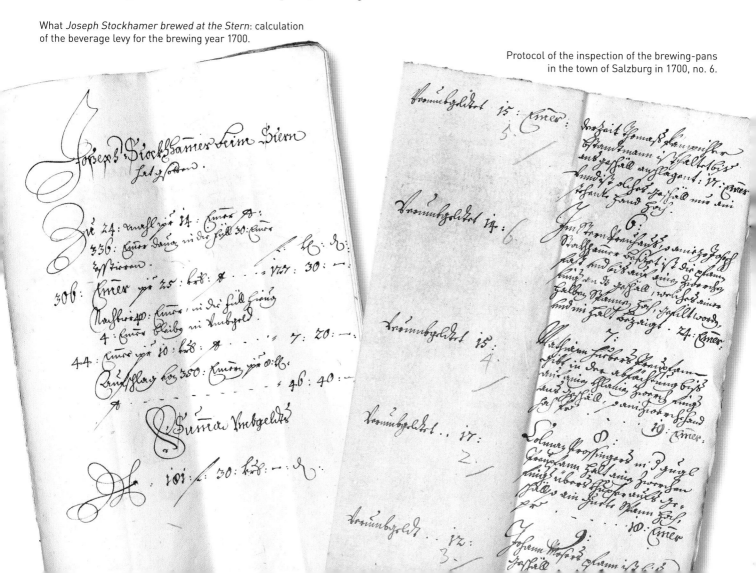

Brewers and Maltsters

As (master) brewers, the proprietors of the *Goldener Stern* belonged to the Salzburg Guild of Brewers and Maltsters. The town and police ordinance decreed in 1524 by Cardinal Matthäus Lang von Wellenburg had fixed the number of Salzburg breweries and suspended the guilds by an order *to be observed henceforth by all guilds and fraternities.*[24] He was less concerned with the general abolition of mandatory guild membership than with bringing the trade guilds and fraternities under the superintendence of the municipal judge, and thus under his control. Under the supervision of the governor and his officials, the guilds nevertheless still functioned as an important instrument for keeping order amongst the corporations in Salzburg's business landscape. By the 16th century, many trades had already established their own guild regulations, and the brewers were amongst the last to formulate standard specifications. The earliest recorded list of regulations for brewers is not for Salzburg, however, but for the trade in Hallein. This ordinance of 1592[25] was not followed by that for Salzburg until 1625, when Carl Dunstler was proprietor of the *Goldener Stern*. Dated 28 February, it was issued and certified in the course of a general trade reformation under Archbishop Paris Lodron.[26] It consists of 29 articles, and regulates such aspects as work contracts, training from apprentice to master and the annual meeting of the guild members, as well as dues and contributions to the craftsman's chest.[27]

To become a master, the craftsman had to produce a "master-piece", the *master-beer*, which was tasted and assessed at the inspection by colleagues, the municipal judge and a delegate from the town council. If it was deemed good, and had no particular deficiencies, the applicant was received as a master, on payment of 10 gulden and two pounds of wax for the craftsman's chest.

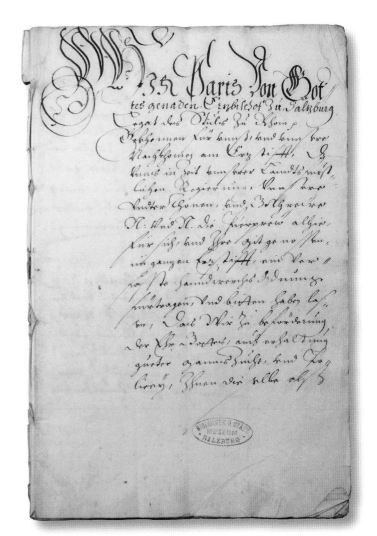

Trade regulations for brewers and maltsters, 1625, transcript from 1627, p 1.

The most important day of the year for the trades was the so-called "Jahrtag" [annual day] held on the feast of Corpus Christi.[28] Traditionally, the day opened with a sung High Mass[29] in St. Michael's Church, intercessions being made to the Virgin Mary and St. Florian, patron of the guilds. Thereafter, from 1 p.m., the guild members held a meeting presided over by the guild master. The

Arrival of a journeyman, welcomed by the host, on a guild picture of the Salzburg Ledererherberge in the Ledererergässchen, oil on wood, 1615 (restored in 1647 and 1770), detail.

brewers and maltsters assembled in their adopted inn; for many years this was the *Stockhamerbräu* which, as mentioned above, had been associated with the Sternbräu since the days of Georg Ehrenreich Stockhamer.[30] In the presence of the municipal judge or his deputy, and a *commissarius* delegated by the mayor, the guild master and deputies were newly appointed, and all current legal matters dealt with "before the open chest".[31] Thus the assembly sat in judgement, and punishments were meted out for contraventions of the guild's code. Decisions were also made on controversial claims. Considerable attention was given to *Aufdingen*, the admission of apprentices, and *Freisprechen*, their qualification upon completion of their apprenticeship. Both of these were accompanied by spe-

cific ceremonies and took place in the presence of at least some non-members of the guild, particularly the parents.[32]

The contributions (6 gulden annually for each master) paid into the guild chest served, besides discharging these occasional liabilities, for the purchase of various items pertaining to the guild, remuneration for clerical work or paying burial costs. The moneys were also used for the "gift", the viaticum for travelling journeymen who came to the town but were given no work, or for the medical care of sick apprentices or journeymen.[33]

When the business of the guild had been dealt with, it was time for the convivial part of the proceedings, with food and drink playing a considerable role.[34] On 12 June 1712, *after work was completed, food and drink to the value of 30 gulden 15 kreutzer were consumed* in the *Stockhamerbräu*,[35] and in 1740, 23 persons dined for 34 gulden 30 kreutzer.[36]

House signs and fire authority

Since the town and police ordinance of 1524, those businesses that required fire in their production process were increasingly regulated throughout the modern period. These trades included especially the brewers, of whom there were twelve in the 17th-century town – three of them in the immediate vicinity of the Getreidegasse. Regulations were frequently prescribed, and inspections carried out. For example, on 13 August 1680, the court councillor ordered that all the brewers, kilns or maltings in the town should be inspected by an expert, with particular attention to fire risk.[37] Calling in experts was intended to ensure that safety hazards were recognised and eliminated as quickly as possible. Parallel to this, building regulations were extended and inspections carried out to ensure compliance – which was not always the case. On 9 May 1691, the *Stern* landlord Georg Ehrenreich Stockhamer was ordered by the manorial court

The old house signs of the *Goldener Stern*

The large house-sign that still projects far into the Getreidegasse dates from the days when Georg Ehrenreich Stockhamer was proprietor of the *Goldener Stern,* in the latter half of the 17th century. It is a particularly ornate cast-iron cantilever, partly gilded. On a triangular bracket with elaborate rocaille ornamentation there hangs, under a baldachin, an open-work lantern containing a fermenting vat with brewing tools. Hanging at the end is a star, framed in rocaille and bearing the abbreviation St. B. (= Sternbräu).

The more recently added ornamental cartouche above the baldachin, with the logo of the Österreichische Brau AG [Austrian Brewing Company], rather mars the overall appearance. The scroll under the star bears the renovation dates 1720 and 2014. This luxuriant decoration gives the sign special prominence in the Getreidegasse.

A second house-sign, considerably more modest and less attention-catching, hangs on the building at Griesgasse 23 (see details on pp 101/102).

House-signs of the Sternbräu in the Getreidegasse and the Griesgasse.

41

to pay a fine of 18 gulden, because he had without permission broken through the town wall behind his garden, started building work and criminally cut off the roof of the walkway.[38]

Stockhamer had often had to struggle with problems, as for instance in August 1675, when he demanded repayment of a debt from Christoph Egedacher, the well-known organ-maker to the archiepiscopal court.[39] The amount in dispute, some 70 gulden, had been incurred for delivery of wine and beer. He had already paid the alcohol levy, Stockhamer protested in a letter to Cardinal Max Gandolf von Kuenburg, and asked him for assistance. Kuenburg thereupon instructed the court treasurer's office to request a written explanation from Egedacher and to report back to him.[40] Egedacher admitted his debt and offered to settle it by payment of one gulden per month, since due to the hard times, a large household and his many children, he could not afford more.[41] Stockhamer refused to accept this offer, however, especially since, as he argued, he, too, had a wife and children to support, and repayment in full could not be guaranteed because he "could not know how long the Lord God would spare Egedacher's life".[42] He demanded a repayment of at least three gulden per month, and Egedacher countered by saying that with his monthly salary of eight gulden, this was impossible.[43] The legal action ended with Egedacher's assurance that he would pay the 70 gulden immediately he had money again. Sources give no indication of when or whether that ever happened.

Letter from Georg Ehrenreich Stockhamer to the Archbishop concerning the outstanding debts of the court organ-maker Christoph Egedacher, August 1675.

Marble plaque on the *Stockhamerbräu* above the portal of the passage to the Getreidegasse, Universitätsplatz 2.

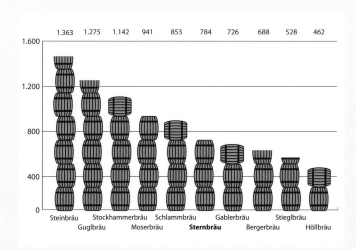

| 1.363 | 1.275 | 1.142 | 941 | 853 | 784 | 726 | 688 | 528 | 462 |

Quantities of beer (in hecto-litres) produced
by ten Salzburg breweries in 1700.

Beer production around 1700

During the 17th century – apart from the hard times of the Thirty Years' War – there was little change in the economic circumstances of the town's breweries. All twelve brewers belonged to the well-to-do citizenry, although there was the occasional case of bankruptcy. The Sternbräu was no exception. Only the archiepiscopal court brewery *Kaltes Brauhaus im Kai*, founded in 1648, had never really got off the ground, and it closed down in 1704.

The beer price fixed in 1692 also remained steady for a century or so.[44] Production figures around the turn of the century show three of the town's breweries leading: Steinbräu, Guglbräu and Stockhamerbräu, each with an annual production of over 1,000 hectolitres. In 1700, the Sternbräu was in the middle bracket with 1,248 buckets, or 784 hectolitres.[45]

Johann Gottfried Graf Lützow, *Vue de la ville capitale de Salzbourg prise du couvent de Maria Plan*, copper engraving, 1789.

In the town of Salzburg, an archiepiscopal seat with a population of some 16,000 towards the end of the 18th century,[1] the taverns attached to the breweries assumed an important role in public life. Patrons went there not only to eat and drink, but to participate in dancing, gaming and general celebration, and the larger saloons – such as that in the *Goldener Stern* – were venues for guild assemblies, wedding receptions, student parties and church occasions, as well as for theatrical performances and variety acts.[2]

The tavern was also a trading-point for wares and services, and letters could be left there for messengers to collect. While there were dance-floors in many of the town's taverns, only a few, such as the *Stern*, had a bowling-alley. In 1804 the Sternbräu even had three – more than any other tavern in Salzburg.

Accommodation for travellers and coaching inn

If the inns served local residents as meeting-places for various forms of entertainment, they were important as overnight accommodation for strangers to the town. If we look for references in contemporary literature, travel writers reporting on Salzburg seem for the most part to have been quite satisfied with the quality and price structure of lodgings in Salzburg; the actual prices were found to be quite acceptable. For instance, in the *few letters on Salzburg* in Theophil Friedrich Ehrmann's *Der Weltbürger* [The cosmopolitan], published in 1792, we read: *The inns, not so many here, are almost all very tolerable; the service is good, and the prices, albeit that everything here*

Stage coach, undated, copper engraving by Sobberer/Kohl, detail.

has been very expensive for some years now, are still fairly humane.[3] In his topography of the town published the following year, Salzburg litérateur and journalist Lorenz Hübner writes: *For travellers and strangers, it is particularly important to know good inns where proper service, comfortable accommodation and decent food can be found … Lodgings for more high-bred travellers include those*

logiert bey der blauen Gans, nimmt Briefe auch Waaren mit nacher Regensburg, und Straubing.

Laufner-Both kommt am Dienstag, Donnerstag und Samstag, ist zu finden bey Herrn Zezi, Kaufmann in der Traidgassen, gehet selbige Täg um 2. Uhr von hier wiederum ab.

Lofer-Both kommt am Donnerstag, gehet am Freytag in der Frühe wiederum ab.

M.

Mattighofer-Both kommt wochentlich zweymal, hat seinen Einsatz bey dem Herrn Baurnfeind, auf dem Kranzelmarkt.

Mattseer-Both kömmt am Donnerstag, und gehet Freytag zwischen 10. und 11. Uhr Mittags wiederum ab, logiert bey dem Freyhammerbräu nächst der St. Andräe-Kirchen.

Mauerkircher-Both kommt alle 14. Täge, hat seinen Einsatz bey dem Herrn Baurnfeind auf dem Kränzlmarkt.

Michaelbaier-Both setzet ein bey dem Schuhmacher Grünzenberger in der Traidgassen, neben der Apothecken, kommt wochentlich zwey- bis dreymal, als Montag, Mittwoch, und Donnerstag Abends anhero, gehet anderten Tags Vormittag wiederum ab.

Mondseer-Both logiert auf dem Plätzel über der Brucken bey dem sogenannten Lasserwirth, kommt am Donnerstag, und gehet Freytag um Mittagszeit wiederum ab.

Müldorfer-Both kehret ein bey dem goldenen Stern in der Traidgassen, kommt am Donnerstag, gehet Freytag um 12. Uhr Nachmittag wiederum ab.

Münchner-Both kommt alle Mittwoch um Mittagszeit allhier an, logiert in der Traidgassen bey dem goldenen Stern, gehet Freytag um 12. Uhr wiederum ab, nimmt Briefe, Paqueter, Ballen, auch unterschiedliche Kaufmannsgüter mit sich.

N.

Neumarkter-Both kommt am Montag, und Freytag, und gehet den anderen Tag darauf gegen Mittag wiederum ab, hat seine Einkehr bey dem Lasserwirth auf dem Plätzel.

Oettin-

List of messengers in the 1774 Salzburg court calendar, p 97.

Around the mid-18th century, this inn boasted not only a capacity of 56 beds, but also a large stable and remise,[5] where travellers' horses could be tended and coaches housed. As time went on, however, there was increasing competition for individual modes of transport.

Stage-coach routes were developed, making travel more comfortable, affordable and easier to plan. Around 1790, one could for instance arrive in Salzburg from Carinthia on Tuesday at about 3 p.m., on Wednesday at about 4 p.m. from Upper and Lower Austria, Tyrol or Italy, and on Thursday at 6 p.m. from Munich.[6]

From the latter half of the 18th century onwards, this development brought to Salzburg more travellers interested simply in sight-seeing and culture – early tourists not on the traditional upper-class Grand Tour. There were also, of course, still the commercial travellers, who often used lodgings rented in the inns not only to stay overnight, but also to store and sell their wares. During the 1780s and '90s, citrus fruits were proffered in the *Höllbräu*, pocket watches in the *Stadttrinkstube*, chocolate and Lyon silk in the *Goldenes Schiff*, and a frequent visitor to the Sternbräu in May was a gardener from Lyon, who sold *all manner of plants, roots, seeds and flower-bulbs of the rarest varieties and finest colours.*[7]

In the latter half of the 18th century the postal service was already well organised. The messengers called at

with Herr Müllbacher in the so-called Eitzenberger house in the Judengasse, Herr Kaserer in the Kaigasse, Herr Eschenbacher in the Milchgässchen, Frau Mödlhammer, and the Sternbräu in the Getreidegasse.[4] Salzburg's prize scout also counts the *Goldener Stern* amongst the twelve best lodging establishments in the town.

Chalvin, Gärtner von Lyon, der allerhand Gattungen von Pflanzen, Würzlein, Saamen, und Zwiebel von Blumen von den seltensten Gattungen und schönsten Farben verkauft, erbiethet einem geehrten Publikum seine Dienste; er führt auch allerley Saamen von Küchengewächsen bey sich. Denjenigen Personen, welche es verlangen, verkauft er die Waare auf Proben, und schmeichelt sich den Beyfall und das gütige Zutrauen der Liebhaber auch für folgende Jahre zu gewinnen. Er hat auch verschiedene Stücke für Naturalienkabinete, und logirt beym Sternbräu.

In der Mayr'schen Buchhandlung ist zu haben: Storchenau Zugaben zur Philosophie der Religion. 5ter und letzter Band. 8. Augsburg 789. 1 Fl. 30 Kr. Nachricht. Maria Viktoria Stegerinn von Augsburg ist allhier angekommen, und erbiethet sich auf erhaltene obrigkeitliche Verwilligung mit ihrer Arbeit alle zerbrochene Frauenzimmer-Fächer zu repariren, und zu überziehen. Sie führet auch zu diesem Ende viele seine Französische und Chinesische Ueberzüge von Papier, Leder und Tafet mit sich, und ist bereit, das hochzuverehrende Publikum mit ihrer Arbeit um sehr billige Preise zu bedienen. Ihr Logis ist im goldenen Stern in der Getreidgasse.

Advertisements in the *Salzburger Intelligenzblatt*, 8 May and 2 October 1790, placed by a gardener from Lyon offering plants for sale, and a woman from Augsburg who repairs ladies' fans. Both put up at the *Goldener Stern*, where they awaited customers.

various Salzburg inns to collect letters and consignments of goods. According to the list in the 1774 Salzburg court calendar, the *Goldener Stern* was the contact point both for the messenger from Mühldorf (a Salzburg enclave in the middle of Bavaria), who arrived on Thursday and set off on the return journey on Friday, and for the Munich messenger, who stayed rather longer at the *Goldener Stern*, arriving around midday on Wednesday but leaving again only on Friday at midday. Besides letters, parcels and bales, messengers would also accept commercial goods for transport.

The *Goldener Stern* – a bankrupt inn?

As previously mentioned, from 1665 the *Goldener Stern* remained for several generations in the possession of the Stockhamer family. Josef Stockhamer, who together with his wife had purchased the tavern and brewery from his brother Georg Ehrenreich Stockhamer in 1702, handed the business over to his son Johann Georg Stockhamer in 1727. On 28 January 1737, the new owner married Maria Anna Wilhelmseder, daughter of the innkeeper and shipowner Johann Wilhelmseder and his wife Maria Stadler from Tittmoning.

Five years later, however, he went spectacularly bankrupt. A significant cause was probably the massive credits which were often carried over from one owner to the next and for which, due to various circumstances, repayments could no longer be met. By June 1741, Stockhamer's existing assets were monetised, to the equivalent of the

Auction decree in the proceedings against the bankrupt *Stern* brewer Johann Georg Stockhamer, 5 April 1742.

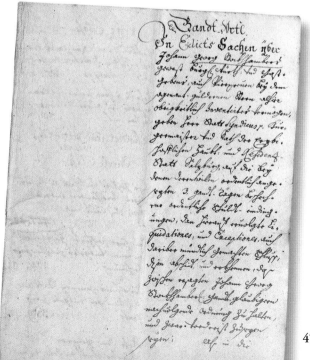

47

substantial sum of 14,000 gulden.[8] Documented in the auction decree[9] by the town syndic, mayor and council were three days on which bids could be handed in. The sale of the brewery and inn was then, however, carried out in a kind of auction.[10] This started with a bid of 16,000 gulden, outbid by 200 gulden, by Joseph Schallhardt on behalf of a client not named in the council protocol. He in turn was outbid to the tune of 100 gulden by Anna Maria Stadler from Tittmoning. Mutual outbidding continued, and finally it was Anna Maria Stadler, mother of the bankrupt's wife, who made the highest bid, on 4 September 1742. She acquired the tavern and the licence for the princely sum of 18,050 gulden, and handed the Sternbräu over to her son Johann Mathias Wilhelmseder.[11] The liquidation of the assets and the high purchase price were nevertheless insufficient to satisfy the demands of the creditors. Stockhamer's debts turned out to be massive: 3,500 gulden were outstanding to Hagenauer's heirs, 2,000 to the *Bürgerspital*, 2,100 to court chancellor Schallhammer, 1,000 to the Order of the Knights of St. Rupert, 2,000 to the collegiate church in Tittmoning, 3,000 to his wife, 1,633 to Anna Maria Stadler, 2,800 to the children of Andree Gräfendorfer, 1,000 to the Augustinian monastery in Mülln, and so on… The debts finally totalled more than 64,000 gulden, so the creditors could be indemnified for only about 50 percent.

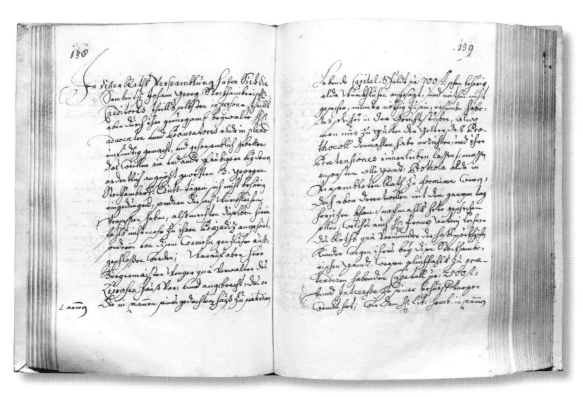

Statt Raths Prothocoll Salzburg de Anno 1741, entry for the session on 8 March 1741 (first two pages).
On this day all the creditors or their representatives met at the municipal court and agreed on further procedure.

The Tittmoning Wilhelmseder family in Salzburg

Several members of this prominent family (resident in Tittmoning since 1615) were present in the town of Salzburg during the 18th century. The most important of these was Kaspar Wilhelmseder (1676–1767), the eldest son of a Tittmoning innkeeper and his wife Elisabetha Peyer.[12] He must have learned the merchant trade in his native town, and at the age of 27 he moved to Salzburg, where he found employment as a salesman in the *Christoph Bergamin'schen Spezerey-Waren-Handlung* [grocery]. On 3 September 1709 he married Magdalena Renate, daughter of his employers Christoph Bergamin and Katharina. Shortly afterwards, on his admission as a citizen on 7 December 1709, Kaspar Wilhelmseder is mentioned as the proprietor of the shop at Judengasse 7, then in 1713 as owner of the house.

Ten years later, at the request of Archbishop Franz Anton Harrach (r. 1709–1727), he was appointed to the town council; from 1732 he was town treasurer, and figured on the 1732 list of mayoral candidates. In 1737 he assumed the office of curator of Salzburg parish church, and when he had stablised the municipal budget, he was appointed tax-collector general in 1740. Finally, in 1741 he was elected mayor, and held this office over the reigns of no less than four archbishops. At the same time, he gained a reputation as money-lender to the prince-archbishops, and on the other hand as a generous patron. He donated not only the side-altar of the *miraculous Virgin* Mary in the parish church (now the Francis-

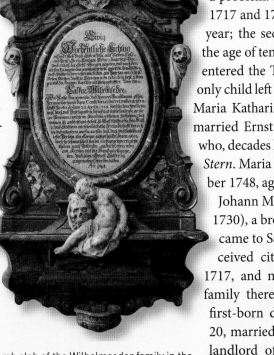

Tomb slab of the Wilhelmseder family in the Hospital Church of St. Blasius, installed under the 1749 endowment.

can Church), but also contributed financially to the pulpit in the Tittmoning collegiate church, executed by Johann Georg Itzlfeldner (1705–1760). In 1747, he commissioned Viennese artist Paul Troger (1698–1762) to execute a new altar painting of the Three Wise Men for the Hospital Church of St. Blasius in Salzburg, where he was allotted a family vault.

In his old age, however, handing over his evidently flourishing grocery business proved a problem. Four children born between 1717 and 1723 each lived for less than a year; the second-born daughter died at the age of ten, and the two surviving sons entered the Tegernsee monastery. So the only child left to take over the business was Maria Katharina; on 23 January 1748 she married Ernst von Antretter (1718–1791) who, decades later, purchased the *Goldener Stern*. Maria Katharina died on 1 December 1748, aged only 35.[13]

Johann Michael Wilhelmseder (1692–1730), a brother of the Salzburg mayor, came to Salzburg to study in 1710, received citizenship in Tittmoning in 1717, and married into an innkeeper's family there. On 28 January 1737, his first-born daughter Maria Anna, aged 20, married Johann Georg Stockhamer, landlord of the *Goldener Stern*, who went bankrupt five years later.[14] The couple had no children, but her mother, Anna Maria Stadler, and her stepfather Peter Paul Stadler acquired the brewery and the inn at the bankruptcy auction and handed it over to their (step)son Johann Mathias Wilhelmseder.

An exceptional career – Johann Mathias Wilhelmseder

Born in Tittmoning in 1720, the third child of Johann Michael Wilhelmseder, Johann Mathias Wilhelmseder moved to Vienna in the autumn of 1738 and worked there as a waiter in the *Goldener Ox*.[15] In 1742, aged 22 and now in Salzburg, he acquired the *Goldener Stern*, handed over to him by his mother. That same year he received citizenship of Salzburg,[16] and on 14 May 1743 he married Sophia Duschl, daughter of a brewer from Lochen, which was then in the Bavarian Innviertel. They had three children,[17] but she died on 1 April 1756, aged 35. Only three months later, on 13 July 1756, he married Maria Franziska Katharina Furthueber (or Forsthuber), daughter of a brewer and wine-tavern keeper who was also mayor of Hallein.[18] Five of the couple's eleven children died within two years of their birth. In 1770, their eldest daughter married Joseph Moshammer, landlord of the *Goldener Hirsch* (Getreidegasse 37); another daughter, Maria Anna, married the court and cathedral musician Mathias Franz de Paula Stadler.

Master brewer and assistant at the brewing-copper: group of figures from the mechanical theatre in the water-garden (1613) in the park at Hellbrunn Palace.

Guild hostelries and "Jahrtag" feasts

In the latter half of the 18th century, Salzburg's trades were divided into 50 guilds,[19] the catering trade being an exception, since it was not organised in guilds but depended on privileges granted by the authorities. The brewers and maltsters, on the other hand, formed a corporation which was for a long time based in the *Stockhamerbräu* (Getreidegasse 35),[20] where they held their meetings. The brewery journeymen were organised into a separate confraternity.[21]

The brewers moved from the *Stockhamerbräu* to the *Stieglbräu in der Gstätten* in 1773. On 1 July 1774 (the guild's annual day), Stiegl brewer Johann Ambros Elixhauser assumed the dual function of innkeeper and incumbent guild-master and treated his colleagues to

game pie, haunch of venison with caper sauce, crabs and smoked tongue, oranges, endive salad and asparagus. For dessert he served cherry-cake, krapfen, ice-cream and almond pancakes or almond gâteau. Apart from beer, there was wine from Austria, Tyrol and Hungary, with coffee and liqueurs to finish.[22]

The journeyman brewers were not to be outclassed; for their festive meal attended in 1740 by 42 persons including the guild-master and a number of women,[23] an incredible spread consisting of 67 chickens, 21 ducks, haunch of venison, game pie, salads and a variety of desserts was prepared. Although the annual celebration was held in a brewery inn, little beer was drunk, but the landlord served 53.4 litres of wine. After this copious feast, musicians played for dancing.

A festive meal, oil on canvas, anonymous, 1726, detail.

The brewer, anonymous copper engraving, 1805, from: The Book of Trades, or Library of the Useful Arts, London 1806/07.

After running the business for two years, landlord Johann Matthias Wilhelmseder came to the conclusion that it would be more useful if he actually understood the brewing trade, so that he could keep an eye on what the journeymen were doing. So although it was unusual in Salzburg for a married man to enter into an apprenticeship, he decided to seek a master. After all, in Bavaria every brewery had to employ a master-brewer – *and anyway, it would be far more praiseworthy for a man to wish to learn a trade than to continue his life in ignorance.*[24] This insight prompted him to apply to the guild for acceptance as an apprentice – a unique occasion in the history of the Salzburg trade. Even the town magistrate pointed out that *we know no case of a married citizen learning a trade as an apprentice and qualifying therein.*[25]

The training process, strictly regulated by the guild, did not allow for this. Admission as an apprentice for two years was subject to precise rules[26]. An applicant had to bring two honourable men to pledge for him, and pay a deposit of 32 gulden from which his master could deduct expenses and pay for any damage done.[27] An apprentice lived and worked in his master's house, the master being *in loco parentis,* so that the apprentice was not permitted to leave the house without the master's knowledge. In Wilhelmseder's case, an additional problem was the compulsory journeying upon completion of the apprenticeship, which had to be certified through documentary evidence.[28]

Although almost all the guild's conditions were inapplicable to him, Wilhelmseder still wished to be admitted. An entry in the town council protocol for 1743 records that Mathias Wilhelmseder, landlord of the *Goldener Stern*, had applied for permission to serve a regular brewing apprenticeship, and to be taken on by a master until such time as he would qualify as a journeyman.[29] The town council, somewhat at a loss, asked the guild members for their opinion. Surprisingly enough, they were unanimous in their decision to raise no objection, and provided a written statement to this effect.[30] They did, however state expressly that during his apprenticeship Wilhelmseder should expect no advantages from his status as citizen and landlord.[31] Accordingly, the town council decided that he should duly learn the brewing trade and be accepted as master when he had fulfilled all the necessary conditions.[32] Between the times of these various statements, however, a great deal of discussion took place, so that it was not until 10 September 1745 that Wilhelmseder entered his apprenticeship under the guild-master Lorenz Hierl (Hörl). After the statutory two years, completed in the neighbouring Stockhamer-brauerei (Getreidegasse 35), on 28 September 1747 he took up his indentures[33] and was received into the trade.[34] The travel period expected of a journeyman was evidently waived, but no written dispensation is to be found in the records.

Wilhelmseder had achieved his aim: he was citizen, innkeeper, and now also an honourable member of the Salzburg guild of brewers and maltsters. Shortly afterwards, he had his portrait painted in oils – self-assured and in dignified pose, resplendent in a dark-brown coat with two waistcoats, the inner one of gold brocade, and a gold-braided black cape. His hair is powdered grey, and

Left: Portrait of brewer Johann Mathias Wilhelmseder, oil on canvas, remounted, artist unknown, 1749.

Entry in the 1743 town council protocol, recording Johann Mathias Wilhelmseder's reception into the trade.

Agreement on the division of the legacy of
Sophia Duschl/Wilhelmseder, 2 April 1757.

bers of the town council, 49 selected citizens had the honour of partaking in this feast. These rare invitations to the archiepiscopal table were highly symbolic occasions, and carried great prestige in the relationship between town elders and citizens.

Dance floor, bowling alley and chapel – the facilities offered by the *Goldener Stern* in the mid-18th century

When Wilhelmseder's first wife, Sophia Duschl, died on 1 April 1756, the customary probate inventory was carried out, covering not only personal effects but also the brewery property and all movable possessions.[37] This shows that at this time the *Goldener Stern* was already one of Salzburg's major inns, and so the high purchase price had been by no means excessive. The garden contained 19 tables and – in keeping with the rising fashion in Salzburg's restaurants during the 18th century – a large pavilion with six wooden tables, one of marble and one of slate.

Altogether 28(!) rooms with a total of 80 tables were available to guests. In the *Sitz*, the public bar, there were seven wooden tables with benches; in most of the other rooms there were fewer, but also with chairs. The smaller rooms each had only one table. The smarter rooms, such as the wedding room or the merchants' room, were furnished with sofas, leather armchairs and pictures, some also with mirrors, cupboards and clocks. The 56 beds listed in the inventory were distributed over almost all the public rooms. One of the few areas furnished with only tables and benches was the dance-floor. Most of the rooms had a bed, some had two, only a few had more; the wedding room and the dance-floor room had three, the snuggery four, the Thällerer room and the former meat store five, St. Peter's room six, and the Haffner chamber eleven. The other furnishings indicate that evidently this

on his left hand, which holds a letter addressed to him, he wears a large cornelian ring.[35]

As a universally respected businessman, around 1750 he was invited to the court Christmas banquet, together with brewers Franz Dietrich Popp and Adam Öxler, and innkeepers Johann Georg Genser, Johann Strobl, Jacob Stainleithner und Johann Mundtigler.[36] Besides 15 mem-

Premises and tables 1756

Catering and accommodation

Public room (5 tables)
General public room
(5 tables)
Merchants' room (4 tables)
Kuchlstube [snuggery]
Pavilion (8 tables)
Garden (19 tables)
Churchmen's room
(1 table)
Back, middle and
front organ rooms
Dining room (1 table)
Social room (3 tables)
St. Paul's room (1 table)

Stern room (5 tables)
Wedding room (1 table)
Count's room (3 tables)
Schällerer room (2 tables)
St. Peter's room (2 tables)
Thällerer room (1 table)
Mitterer chamber
Piding room (2 tables)
Haffner chamber
and antechamber
Dance-floor room (1 table)
Dance floor (several tables)
Public bar (7 tables)
Bodenstüberl [loft]
Wagoners' room (3 tables)
Welsches Stübl

[Southerners' room]
Fleischkammer (former
meat store)

Utility rooms, private and staff rooms

Bedrooms/private
Women's room
Children's room
Hänner room (with scales
for weighing fish)
Kitchen
Old kitchen
Larder
Bread store
Wood-loft

Hay-loft
Brewery workers' room
Shed
Brew- and mash-house
Upper pantry
Chapel and sacristy
Manservants' room
Cheese vault
Still-house
Beer cellar
Wine cellar
Coach house
Tool-shed
Stables
Barn

last room, including a side-room with three more beds, were the only ones used exclusively as bedrooms, while all the other rooms were multi-functional, used for eating and drinking as well as for overnight stays. The most elegant bedroom was the Count's room, which boasted a four-poster with green curtains.

A unique feature among the Salzburg inns was the *Goldener Stern*'s private chapel with sacristy, installed by Wilhelmseder. It was on the first floor of the low-rise wing (demolished in 1930/31)[38] which separated the two gardens and connected what is now the Griesgasse with the houses on the Getreidegasse. Mass was celebrated several times a year in the chapel.[39]

Besides this small sacred area, exceptional for a tavern, there was the large secular one with the brewery and the inn, including the mash-house with malting-floor, stabling, etc. The beer-brewing equipment was worth some 400 gulden. Then there was of course the beer-cellar, a barn for storing a variety of wood, empty beer and wine barrels, buckets, iron hoops and much more, as well as several smaller rooms such as the tool-shed and a shed containing, amongst other things, the grindstone – essential for the cooks. Stables and a coach-house were used by visitors, as well as for the inn's own vehicles, ranging from cart to carriage.

The working premises of the inn included two kitchens equipped with the usual cooking utensils, two pantries where crockery and glasses were also stored, a small room containing copper scales for weighing fish, and separate store-rooms for bread, meat and cheese.

The Sternbräu chapel

The altar at the front end of the chapel had a superstructure with sculptures, wood and stucco, and was framed by Ionic columns and pilasters and the two wooden figures of St. Florian and St. George.[40] The altar painting, by an unknown 18th-century artist, showed the Crucifixion.

Besides paintings of scenes from the life of the Virgin, the martyrdom of St. Vitus and an unknown priest, the side wall bore a large oil portrait (88 x 118 cm) of the seated Archbishop Sigismund Christoph Schrattenbach (1753–1771). The letter in his hands showed the words: *Decretum an Johann Matthias von Wilhelmseder burgerl. Weingastgeb. und Bierbräu beym goldenen Stern allhier de dato 27. Juni 1755* [decree to Johann Matthias von Wilhelmseder, wine-tavern keeper and beer brewer at the *Goldener Stern* here, on 27 June 1755], which provides an indication of the date when the chapel was built. A series of wooden figures – putti, angels, the saints Christopher, Rochus, John the Baptist, John the Divine, Elizabeth and Ulrich – dated from the latter half of the 16th century. In addition, the chapel was furnished with two procession poles, two red marble stoups with skull and crossbones, and two rows of pews.[41] There was even a small organ, which explains why the adjoining rooms in the inn were called the back, middle and front organ rooms.

While an 1897 travel guide states that "the middle building contains a very old, interesting private chapel", the *Salzburger Volksblatt* reported in 1925 that several art-works had disappeared between 1918 and 1922.[42] This was the period when the Sternbräu AG had sold the original building in the Old Town in 1918, then re-acquired it at the beginning of 1925 and then in two stages, 1926 and 1930/31, carried out the first complete renovation of the entire building. In the process, the wing containing the chapel was totally demolished. Even before the sale, however, there had been initial ideas for reconstruction, when the Sternbräu AG informed the provincial conservator, on 12 March 1914, that the chapel was housed in an inferior building which, *like the entire Sternbräu property with its stabling, old brewery and maltings would sooner or later have to be demolished.*[43] Thereupon both parties expressed the opinion that the chapel "should in its entirety be preserved in a suitable place". Max Ott, the mayor of Salzburg, immediately declared himself ready *to make available from municipal funds a considerable sum for the purchase for the museum, if the remainder of the purchase price can be raised from state funds.* The Monuments Office agreed, but considered the price of 16,000 kronen demanded by the Stern AG excessive, in view of the fact that the quality of the figures, according to the officials in Vienna, *could only be described as handicraft.* The conservator's effort to negotiate a reduction of the overall price were evidently unsuccessful, and the last existing private chapel in the town of Salzburg was apparently scattered to the winds, little by little.

The whereabouts of the majority of the furnishings can no longer be determined. Before the chapel was demolished, two life-size wooden figures were taken to St. Peter's Abbey[44] – or rather, back to St. Peter's, for the saints Wolfgang and Leonhard, which date from the latter half of the 16th century, can be identified from a copper engraving: part of a side altar created by Hans Waldburger in 1625, they stood beside the high altar columns.[45]

Today, the two figures stand in the new Salzburg DomQuartier, a museum round tour opened in 2014. The former St. Leonhard, a 1.7m-high lime-wood sculpture, was transformed by an alteration of the attribute into a St. Benedict; the polychromy is well preserved and the habit is gilded (pectoral and chalice, however, are modern additions). The fine shaping of the face and hands, the deep folds of the habit, linked by cross-webs, and the modelling of the thigh of the free leg all testify to fine craftsmanship. Similarly the figure of St. Wolfgang, transformed into St. Rupert by alteration of the individual attributes. At least one St. Christopher and an angel from the Sternbräu chapel, which have been lost, were probably part of the St. Peter's altars.

Saints Leonhard (now Benedict) and Wolfgang (now Rupert) from the Sternbräu chapel (previously from St. Peter's Abbey), displayed since 2014 in the Salzburg DomQuartier.

Cost estimate of the individual objects of the chapel furnishings, 30 December 1926.

Details concerning the amount of grain stored and the number of barrels of wine give at least an approximate idea of the size of the catering business. The reserves of grain were estimated at 3,448 gulden, and those of malt for the brewery at 2,277 gulden. This amount of capital alone could have bought a small tavern in Salzburg, such as the *Zirkelwirtshaus* (now Pfeifergasse 14).[46]

The wine reserves were also considerable, with Italian (216 gulden) and Tyrolean (572 gulden) far surpassed by a variety of Austrian wines (2,596 gulden) – making a total of 3,384 gulden in wine alone (spirits to the value of 50 gulden being of no consequence). The high value of the stocks is also evident in comparison with the estimate of the furnishings and movables of the *Goldener Stern*, which totalled only 1,607 gulden. In 1756, the stocks of grain and wine were the largest item (59.2 percent) in the calculated total capital of 11,539 gulden (34,112 gulden assets minus 22,573 gulden liabilities). The level of debt was high, but evidently not (yet) alarming.

Long-term tenants in the *Goldener Stern*

In the larger Salzburg catering establishments, besides the public rooms, there were also rooms for private use, as well as long-term rented accommodation (usually in the upper storeys) – but the 1756 Sternbräu inventory gives no information about this. One indication comes from Leopold Mozart in a letter to his wife dated 20 February 1770, concerning plans for moving house: *So you must write and tell me whether we should lodge at the Sailerwirt, the Stern or the Saulentzl.*[47] We learn more from a census carried out in 1794, which gives details of the occupants of all the houses in Salzburg, district by district. The number of permanent residents in the inns – counting the owner and his family, servants and tenants – varied widely, ranging from four persons in *Krimpelstätter*, eight in the *Stadttrinkstube*, 12 each in the *Eizenberger*, *Löchlwirt*, *Berger-* and *Kasererbräu*, 13 in the *Guglbräu* and *Zirkelwirtshaus*, 15 in the *Höllbräu*, 16 in the *Mödlhamerbräu*, 18 in the *Stockhammerbräu*, 21 in the *Gasthof zu den drei Mohren*, 24 in the *Goldenes Schiff*, 27 in the *Weisse* and 33 in the *Schwarzes Rössl*, to 42 in the *Elefant* and 45 in the *Goldene Sonne*.[48] Only four Salzburg inns had over 50 permanent residents: the *Stiegl* houses (*Stiegl=Bäcker=Haus*, *Stiegl=Bräu=Haus* and *Stiegel=Garten=Haus*), which accommodated 58 persons, the *Goldener Stern* buildings (the *Sternbräuhaus* with 38 and the *Sternbräuhaus Stökl* with 23 occupants, making 61), the *Sailerwirtshaus* with 62 and the *Weisses Lamm* with 73 occupants.[49]

Prominent patrons: the Mozart family

Besides the brewery taverns, there were many public houses in Salzburg with a variety of licences to serve alcohol. In 1764 the town had two town cooks, twelve brewery taverns, 14 beer taverns, 29 wine taverns and two coffee-houses.[50] We know from their correspondence that the Mozart family – who had finally not taken lodgings in any of the inns mentioned, but had moved into the "dancing master's house" on the Hannibalplatz (now Makartplatz) – frequented various hostelries, including the *Seilerwirtshaus* by the Löchlbogen (now Hagenauerplatz) directly opposite their first apartment in Getreidegasse 9. From their new apartment they often went to the nearby *Hofwirt* in the Bergstrasse, which was known as the "local" for court musicians. The remarks in the Mozart family's letters about drinking beer and wine do not refer to Salzburg hostelries, but only to those visited on their travels. Although they hardly men-

Right: Familie Mozart, oil painting by Johann Nepomuk della Croce, winter 1780/81.

tion Salzburg beer,[51] they do frequently comment on local breweries and their owners. Of the twelve brewery taverns in the town, ten are mentioned by name in the Mozarts' letters.[52]

They often visited the *Goldener Stern*, two minutes on foot from their apartment in the Getreidegasse, to meet friends and acquaintances (*then to the Stern to visit Frau von Paradis…*[53]). Wolfgang Mozart even had a rendezvous there with an admirer, as a letter written by his fa-

ther on 23 October 1777 reveals: *Tell Wolfgang that the big-eyed Mundbecken [baker's] daughter, who danced with him at the "Stern" and often paid him such friendly compliments, and then finally entered a nunnery in Loretto, has returned to her father's house again.*[54] This was the eldest daughter of Johann Georg Feyerl (*c* 1715–1805), baker to the court, a wealthy man who owned, besides two houses on the Platzl, a farm in Riedenburg-Maxglan and a mill in Mülln. Maria Ottilie (1755–1796) tried

to discourage her beloved Wolfgang Mozart from setting out on his projected journey to Augsburg and Paris in September 1777. When she failed to do so, she entered the Loreto convent as a novice, but did not stay the course for long. Although after his journey Mozart tried to persuade her to return to the convent, she refused. She remained unmarried, and died at the age of 41.[55]

Crisis years and renewed bankruptcy

In 1764, Archbishop Sigismund von Schrattenbach instructed the court council to carry out a survey amongst the town's business-owners. The innkeepers were asked, among other things, to assess the economic situation of

their premises.[56] Their statements showed no consistent trend, but critical comments were preponderant. Complaints included the increasing tax burden,[57] the evidently numerous "unofficial" taverns and stiff competition in general within the town. *It's impossible to make a living, because there are far too many*,[58] lamented tavern-keeper Anton Schmierl. The protocol contains no statement from Johann Mathias Wilhelmseder – in contrast to most of his colleagues – on how his business was going. He mentions, apart from the purchase of the property by his mother, his annual dues: 15 gulden tax, 1 gulden *Pannschilling* [excise] for the brewhouse, to be paid to the court treasury, and 4 ½ gulden for the licence to serve wine.[59] There is no mention of the alcohol levy, which was considerably higher.

In addition to the tax burden, the brewers and innkeepers soon had to contend with serious economic slumps. They were worst affected by the agrarian crisis of 1770–1772, when freak weather conditions such as continuous rain or summer snow on the Alpine meadows[60] caused harvest failures over all of Central Europe, resulting in a sudden rise in food prices. The situation was exacerbated by speculators and pestilence. For want of grain, nearly all the Salzburg bakeries and breweries had to close down. In view of these adverse circumstances, the brewers and innkeepers received permission from the authorities to import barley and even beer from abroad,[61] in order to keep their businesses going somehow. The agrarian

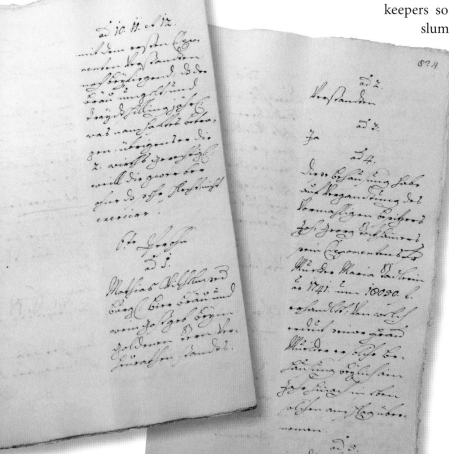

Protocol of the questioning of Johann Mathias Wilhelmseder in the course of the 1764 survey of Salzburg business-owners, no. 4: statement on the purchase of the *Goldener Stern* by his mother.

crisis, however, led to a decrease in the purchasing power of the townspeople, and many customers stayed away. Thus the brewers and innkeepers soon found themselves struggling to earn a living; many of them lost the struggle and slid into bankruptcy. So it was, not only for Wilhelm Elixhauser, owner of the *Gablerbräu*, but also for Johann Mathias Wilhelmseder.[62] Like the Sternbräu and the *Gablerbräu*, several of the smaller businesses had to be sold or auctioned; others were closed down or declared suspended.[63]

Due to the economic slump since 1770, the Sternbräu owner's debt level had mounted to 50,000 gulden, making bankruptcy inevitable.[64] The buildings were advertised to the highest bidder, and the movables were to be sold either as a whole or piecemeal.[65] By public notice and in newspaper advertisements, a *Licitations Day* was announced for 27 July 1772,[66] when bids could be made until the last stroke of 4 p.m.[67] Johann Ernst Edler von Antretter – Salzburg war councillor and secretary to the landed gentry – and his wife made the highest bid: 25,500 gulden, payable in two instalments: 10,000 gulden within four weeks, the rest a year later.[68] This was the highest price paid for a Salzburg brewery and inn before the secularisation of Salzburg in 1803. In addition, Antretter made a bid in writing of 6,000 gulden for the entire fittings and furnishings.[69]

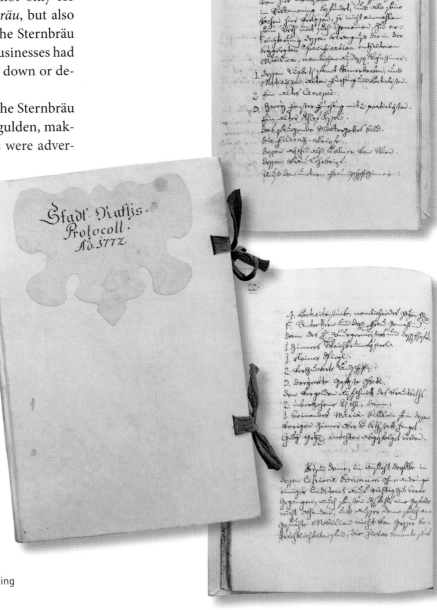

Town council protocol, 1772, pp 21/22:
Mathias Wilhelmseder's request to send on to Tittmoning the personal effects he had left behind in Salzburg.

Even before the auction, Wilhelmseder had returned to his parents' house in Tittmoning. This had evidently been rather too hasty, for he later asked the Salzburg town council to separate out his personal effects from the bankruptcy assets, since he *had left all his things here, and not even taken his bed with him*.[70] This request was granted, and he expressed his sincere gratitude in a letter.[71] In the *enclosed specification* he listed numerous items of furniture which he wished to have sent to him: his bed, an old sofa, two curtains, an old easy-chair, two pictures of Our Lady, letters of indulgence, a holy water basin, two small tables and a few other objects. His brewer's apprenticeship certificate had also been left in Salzburg, as well as his letter of release from his employment as a waiter in Vienna.[72] Amongst the pictures he requested were also four portraits of two married couples: one showed Ignaz Anton Weiser (1701–1785), dramatist and dialect poet, just elected mayor, with his wife; another Johann Ernst von Antretter, purchaser of the bankruptcy assets, with his second wife Maria Anna Elisabeth (1730–1796), daughter of the younger sister of the former mayor Kaspar Wilhelmseder, who had died on 7 November 1755 (see above). This demonstrates that, particularly in the Salzburg catering world, family networks played an important role.

Johann Ernst von Antretter

Johann Ernst von Antretter (1718–1791), a native of Grabenstätt, in Bavaria, came to Salzburg in his youth and received an academic education. He studied jurisprudence at the Benedictine university, began his civil service career in 1745 as a court councillor's assistant, and two years later was promoted to secretary. By way of a post as Assistant Master of the Hunt he achieved the rank of court councillor, religious deputation secretary and privy conference actuary. Elevated to the imperial peerage on 1 December 1756, as "Antretter Edler von Antrettern", in 1758 he became war councillor and secretary to the landed gentry.

Antretter and his family were amongst the Mozarts' close friends, and Anna Maria Mozart ("Nannerl"), in particular, paid frequent visits to Frau Antretter. Besides the so-called Antretter Serenade (K185), composed for the end of the academic year at Salzburg University,[73] Wolfgang Mozart composed the Divertimento in D major (K205), which was often supposed to celebrate the name-day or birthday of Maria Anna Elisabeth Antretter, but which, according to another, perfectly convincing interpretation was intended for Johann Ernst von Antretter's promotion to the post of Assistant Master of the Hunt; this theory may be borne out by the prominence of the two horns in the trio of Minuet II.[74]

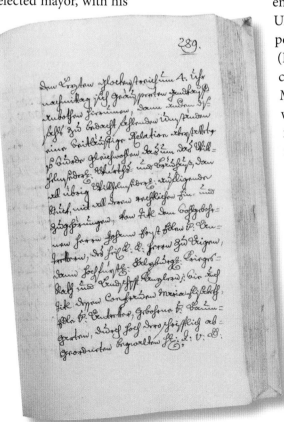

Town council protocol with the entry of guardi2 September 1772, in which the town syndic confirms the purchase of the *Goldener Stern* by Johann Ernst von Antretter and his wife Maria Anna Elisabeth, p 289.

Johann Ernst von Antretter was wealthy; he owned the house at Judengasse 7, purchased Schloss Aigen, and in 1765 also the *Rehlingen Stadtpalais* (now Mozartplatz 4), before acquiring the *Goldener Stern* at auction in 1772. His rather confusing family connection with Wilhelmseder was the result of several circumstances: Antretter was the foster-son and heir of an uncle of the bankrupt, grocer and mayor Kaspar Wilhelmseder (1741–1755), whose daughter Maria Katharina Wilhelmseder (1713–1749) he had married on 23 January 1748. Shortly after her early death, on 21 October 1749 he married her cousin Maria Anna Elisabeth (1730–1796), daughter of the merchant Sebastian Baumgartner and his wife Maria Anna, younger daughter of Kaspar Wilhelmseder. In 1756, upon the death of Maria Josepha Wilhelmseder, landlady of the *Goldener Stern*, he assumed – together with Peter Paul Stadler, mayor of Tittmoning – the guardianship of her four children aged between four and twelve years.

After Antretter's purchase of the insolvent business, the Salzburg economy recovered somewhat in 1773 from the disastrous crisis years and many bankruptcies, but the situation in the catering industry did not improve significantly. This was due partly to competition – the 1774 tax records show 39 wine and beer taverns and 14 small alehouses – and partly to the dual taxation on beer.

Like all the town's inns, the Sternbräu was also affected by negative long-term trends. Whereas in most regions there was a renewed rapid increase in population after the agrarian crisis, both town and Province showed a continuing decrease. The wave of price increases had ruined not only Wilhelmseder's livelihood, but also that of many other Salzburgers, as well as bringing a rapid reduction in the number of marriages.[75] During the ensuing years, the death-rate far exceeded the birth-rate[76] – and food prices continued to rise.[77] Even in economically hard times, however, employees still had to be paid. The

Coat of arms from the copy of the conferment of noble status on Johann Ernst Edler von Antretter, 26 January 1757.

staff and the annual salaries in the *Goldener Stern* are listed in the 1773 census: *Cajetan Antretter, housekeeper 50 gulden; manservant 36 gulden; labourer 30 gulden; Sebastian, houseboy, 20 gulden; head waiter 24 gulden; under-waiter 20 gulden; cook 18 gulden; serving-maid 10 gulden; kitchen-maid 9 gulden.*[78]

Wine and beer taverns in the mid-1770s

Bei den drei Mohren, Goldene Sonne, Goldener Zirkel, Stadttrinkstube, Beim Elefanten, Kaltes Bierhaus, Wirtshaus im Milchgässchen, Beim goldenen Länzl, Beim weissen Löwen, Horner Wirtshaus, Goldener Hirsch, Blaue Gans, Wirtshaus in der Gstätten, Wirtshaus beim Straupp und Schlamm zu Mülln, Wirtshaus im Nonntal, Hammerwirtshaus, Wirtshaus in der Schiessstatt, Wirtshaus beim Lodronschen Regenbogen, Beim blauen Hecht, Bei der goldenen Rose, Beim halben Mondschein, Beim schwarzen Rössl, Beim weissen Rössl, Wirtshaus des Joseph Wilfling, Bei der goldenen Traube, Beim weissen Lamm, Beim goldenen Ochsen, Beim goldenen Engel, Brauwirtshaus im Stein, Goldener Kreuzwirt, Beim goldenen Adler, Beim goldenen Stern, In der Höll, In der Kugel, Beim Türkenkopf, Stockhamerbräu, Im Stagl, Wirtshaus des Joseph Schalhard, Gablerbräu; kleine Bierschenken: *Wirt im Kalten Bräuhaus, Wirt beim Bierfall, Päpäwirt, Wirt im Löchl, Prunerwirt, Pernwirt, Hasenwirt, Beim Kierl, Bettelumkehrwirt, Peterlwirt, In der Pelzhütte, Beim roten Ochsen, Beim Besenstil, Im Ochsenstall.*

Source: SLA, Geheimes Archiv XXVII/22, *Designation Welchergestalten der allhiesige Stadt=Magistrat, Handelsstand, wie auch übrige Bürgerschaft, dann Inwohner, und andere in betref der zu allgemeinen Landes Beÿhilf vor seyend= und auf Vier Jahr lang, nemlich pro Annis 1773. 1774. 1775. et 1776. bestimten Extra ordinari Steuer beleget worden seynd,* 8. Apr. 1774.

By way of comparison: annual living costs for a two-person household in the town of Salzburg at the time amounted to 400 gulden.

Tax burden

If we look back, we see that the introduction of the alcohol levy and in 1664 of the "beer restriction" had placed crippling limitations on the economic administration of the brewers and innkeepers. After further restrictive edicts were issued by Archbishop Jakob Ernst Liechtenstein (1745–1747), the brewers protested vigorously, and finally the authorities and tradesmen agreed on a fixed rate for alcohol tax, the so-called *Komposition.* After a long and tenacious debate, they compromised on a collective annual payment of 12,500 gulden[79] by all the town's breweries together. Figuring in the Salzburg tax register, which lists all the revenue from alcohol levies from 1742 until 1792, are all the *Stern* owners during these 50 years: Johann Georg Stockhamer, Johann Mathias Wilhelmseder, Johann Ernst von Antretter and finally Lorenz Hörl (Hierl, Hirll). Up to 1746, there are the quarterly tax payments on beer, amounting to between 177 and 197 gulden per year; there follows a brief indication of the introduction of the *Komposition.* Not until mid-1777 is there a further change, this time to the former system of individual accounting, until in 1792 the fixed-rate tax is re-introduced for six years.[80]

Hieronymus Colloredo (r. 1772–1803), the last Salzburg prince-archbishop to exercise secular rule, had repealed the *Komposition* agreement which his predecessors had repeatedly extended by several years, hoping for increased revenue from the earlier method of calculation according to the actual amount produced by the

brewers. He aimed to achieve a standard assessment basis by ordering visitations and calibration of the brewing-coppers, and on 23 August 1774 he issued a new beer levy.[81]

In addition to this levy, between 1775 and 1789 Colloredo imposed an excise duty,[82] which resulted in a doubling of the tax – and of course cost the Archbishop further loss of support among the brewers. After several urgent petitions, in 1778 they finally managed to persuade him to reduce the fixed-rate levy of 14,000 gulden to 10,000 gulden;[83] the excise, however, remained.

In addition to this dual tax burden, there were individual complaints and skirmishes among the competitors in the catering industry. In 1779, for instance, the brewer and wine-tavern keeper Josef Mödlhammer and associates complained to the court council that Antretter's stable in the Sternbräu grounds posed an extreme fire risk, and that he refused to do anything about it.[84] No preventive measures were taken, however, and similar complaints were frequently repeated.

Only nine years after they had bought the *Goldener Stern*, Johann Ernst von Antretter and his wife re-sold the property, probably because it was making a loss. On 14 November 1781, Kordula Hierlin (Hörl) purchased the *Goldener Stern*. The Hieronymus land register, kept from 1779 onwards,

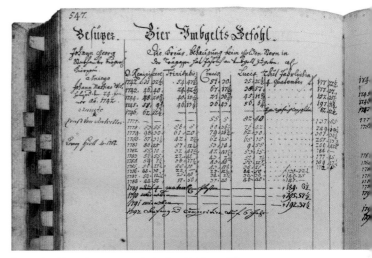

Records of beer levy payments by the *Goldener Stern*, 1742–1792 in the archiepiscopal tax register, p 547.

Alcohol levy imposed by Archbishop Hieronymus Colloredo, 23 August 1774, title page.

provides the information that with a contract dated 14 November 1781, she purchased the property and the business for 20,500 gulden, signifying a loss of 5,000 gulden in the market value within only nine years.[85]

After Kordula Hörl died in 1788, her husband, Franz Hörl, ran the business, at first on his own (although sources mention their son Laurenz as having a share), then with his second wife, Kunigunde Pöstl,[86] who is named as sole owner after his death in 1793.

One thing was abundantly clear: towards the end of the century, the heyday of the *Goldener Stern* – and indeed, of the entire Salzburg catering industry – was over. Taxes and economic slumps, population decline and loss of purchasing power led to the above-mentioned negative consequences, so that even some years before Franz Hörl's death, Lorenz Hübner (in his topography of Salzburg) described this inn – which around mid-century had been a flourishing concern – merely as *the formerly very famous Wilhelmseder wine tavern* (!) *at the sign of the Goldener Stern*.[87]

French occupancy

The Napoleonic Age prolonged the difficult situation, and brought new pressures for Salzburg's citizens and innkeepers. Over the years 1795–1805, an already dwindling population decreased further by over 6 percent.[88] From 1789 onwards, countless reports of the French Revolution, and later of the Napoleonic Wars, reached Salzburg – where there were stirrings of sympathy for the Revolution. Soon *nocturnal disturbances* were reported, and open declarations – mostly from journeymen and students – of the ideas behind the Revolution.[89] Archbishop Hieronymus Colloredo expected an insurrection, and feared expulsion – not by the enemy, but by his own subjects.[90] In 1797, the students began to carry "revolution" cudgels around with them. On 9 February 1798, the municipal judge informed the rector's office of the students' behaviour in the public houses and of the violation of public safety occasioned by the gangs they formed.[91] Since it was to be feared that a violent and deadly affray would soon break out between students and tradesmen, the rector was requested to prohibit the carrying of these cudgels. As a preventive measure, the closing time for all the town's inns and taverns was

French soldiers carousing in the cloister of St. Peter, 1809, watercolour, artist unknown, mid-19th century.

brought forward, in the hope of suppressing tirades against the government and expressions of discontent.

Napoleon's victory at Marengo on 14 June 1800 brought an increasing threat of secularisation of the archbishopric. On 1 July, five months before he was forced to flee Salzburg, Archbishop Hieronymus Colloredo reacted with a final decree aimed at securing law and order. Innkeepers and coffee-house proprietors were instructed to pay heed to *moderation and restraint in political discussions* on their premises. In order to *reduce as far as possible the occasions for such political discussions … at the approach of the enemy, all taverns and coffee-houses shall henceforth without exception be closed at 10 in the evening.*[92]

Enemy troops were indeed coming rapidly closer, and on 15 December 1800 the town of Salzburg was occupied by the victorious French forces.[93] In 1803 Salzburg, now secularised, was handed over in compensation to the Habsburg Duke Ferdinand of Tuscany, as an electorate. There followed several changes of sovereignty, which meant for the entire population burdensome levies of high war contributions and increasing breakdown of central urban functions, until the somewhat reduced territory of Salzburg finally became a permanent part of Austria.[94]

Annoying neighbours or imminent fire risk?

The *Tabular Survey of All Buildings in the Capital Town of Salzburg*, drawn up in 1800/1801 for the introduction of house-numbering, gives two buildings as belonging to the *Goldener Stern*: the *Stern Bräuer Haus* and the *Altes Stern Haus*.[95] While these remained largely unaltered, around the turn of the 18th century there was some building activity in the garden area – the authorities and owners of adjoining properties keeping an eye on potential fire risks. Similarly the neighbours when, for in-

stance, in 1791 town councillor and merchant Felix Raimund Atzwanger (1742–1804) wanted to convert the Sternbräu riverside barn he had purchased into a coachhouse; this was finally authorised, subject to several requirements, such as a minimum distance from the neighbouring walls, a drain, installation of railings, etc.[96]

Problems arose in the spring of 1804. On 11 April, the *concerted neighbours of the Sternbräu garden* reported angrily to the electoral government that the large gate leading from the Badergässchen and Sterngässchen into the Sternbräu garden was "barricaded" to half its height by a wooden wall. They asked for this access to be re-opened as soon as possible, for safety reasons, since there was insufficient space in the narrow Getreidegasse to allow jets of water from the fire-hoses to arc up to the rooftops. This would be possible from the Sternbräu garden, the neighbours maintained, but only if the gate to

Tabular Survey of all buildings in the Capital Town of Salzburg, including the two suburbs of Mülln and Nonnthal …, 1802.

the garden were open, and not, as was currently the case, obstructed by a wooden wall. There was a bowling alley in the garden, in front of the gate; the neighbours, aiming slightly below the belt, went on to complain that *the entire neighbourhood was deprived of this means of help just for the entertainment of those gambling-addicted idlers, most of them low characters – which could perfectly well be moved to the other side of the garden, below the walkway on the town wall.*[97] Besides the *arbitrary obstruction of this gate*, the neighbours pointed out the stables, which were an extreme fire risk since *no-one refrained from smoking tobacco, candles were used at night, and broken lanterns were more likely to be dangerous than*

safe. In a letter dated 8 March 1804, Kunigunda Hörl, proprietor of the *Goldener Stern*, thereupon informed the authorities that as far as the garden was concerned, she had acquired that part of the town wall and the tower in open auction. She had, however, just re-sold the tower and part of the walkway to the town's master carpenter Andree Kern, and on the remaining part of the walkway she intended to build stabling and an apartment. She hereby applied for authorisation for this plan.

Only a year after the secularisation of Salzburg and payment of considerable contributions, Kunigunda Hörl – evidently still solvent – took advantage of her neighbours' petition to obtain, in return for her co-operation, a building permit, for which she repeated her request on 2 June 1804. But the mills of the electoral government ground slowly. A joint on-site inspection was appointed for 2 November 1804, attended in person by Hieronymus von Kleinmayrn, town magistrate and director of police.[98] Also summoned, besides Johann Burgmair, actuary and police under-commissioner, and representatives of the neighbours,[99] were town councillor and master mason Christian Zezi, master bricklayer Mathias Kerlsdorfer, master carpenter Andree Kern and master sweep Franz Xaver Simoni. First of all, it was confirmed and entered in protocol that – as was evident to all – the large entrance-gate to the *Stern* garden was in fact barricaded with wooden planks and

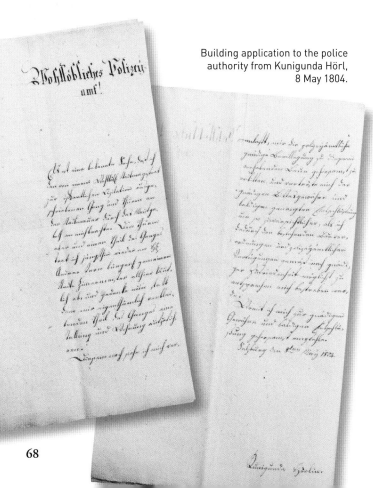

Building application to the police authority from Kunigunda Hörl, 8 May 1804.

that, as the neighbours had asserted, there was a "wall-bowling"[100] alley behind it. The commission of experts, who agreed with the neighbours' criticism, pointed out that the Sternbräu had anyway two other bowling alleys. In view of the potentially serious damage which, in the case of fire, would be inevitable due to the blocked gate, the owner was ordered to remove this obstruction within the space of eight days. Kunigunda Hörl undertook to do this. Attention was then turned to her building application and the existing section of almost 1.80m-thick town wall on the right-hand side (as seen from the entrance), which extended 34 metres – the entire length of the garden. On this wall was a covered walkway where a variety of equipment was stored. For the planned premises, no further wall was intended – only eight pier arches and nine pillars. A staircase would lead up to two heatable rooms, with access to a large unheated room towards the Badergässchen. Finally, the building experts raised no objections to the plans. An amendment dated 21 May 1805 stated that for the inspection the previous year a ground plan had been demanded and submitted, but a stable was now planned instead, and permission for this was requested. With certain stipulations (brick or cement flooring, vault), the experts approved this application.

Kundigunda Hörl ran the *Goldener Stern* for five further years, after which Mathias Waldherr and Anna Holzner purchased the business for 25,000 gulden on 9 May 1810.

Inn sign, probably Sternbräu in the 19th century.

The first two decades of the 19th century brought turbulent times for Salzburg and its population. The entire continent was at a turning-point in history. The former archbishopric became a pawn in the games of the major powers, and the people were expected to put up with a great deal. Salzburg as an independent principality vanished from the map; it was occupied three times by the French, was part of Austria, then of Bavaria, and finally back in Austria. A constant economic, cultural and demographic decline brought town and Province to a marginal status from which they took several decades to recover.

For the brewing business, the 19th century brought an epoch of change and upheaval, with the slow decline of manual production processes and the rise of an industry led by a few large breweries. First of all, the "beer restriction" decreed by the prince-archbishops was abolished in 1808, during the first period of Austrian rule, suddenly confronting the 88 beer-brewers in Salzburg town and Province with the opportunity and challenge of serving their product not only to customers in their own inns, but of selling it to other hostelries and publicans. The former court breweries were gradually auctioned off. That same year, the Hofbrauhaus in Henndorf was transferred to private ownership,[1] followed in 1812 by those in Teisendorf[2] and Lofer.[3] Finally, in December 1815, the Hofbräu Kaltenhausen was sold to the *enfant terrible* of the Bavarian court, the widowed Electress Maria Leopoldine.

During Bavarian rule in Salzburg (1810–1816) the authorities attempted, by means of various edicts and incentives, to persuade the Salzburg brewers to brew according to Bavarian stipulations, converting their operations from the top-fermented to the bottom-fermented brewing process. However, it took several years – until Salzburg was already well and truly part of Austria – for bottom-fermented beers to be accepted in Salzburg.[4]

When Salzburg finally became part of the Austrian Empire, on 1 May 1816, it meant a renewed decline for the economy. Stripped of court, regional government and developed industry, Salzburg became merely a provincial town. For Austria and Habsburg economic policy, peripheral Salzburg had no economic significance whatever. Crop failures in 1814–1816 led to a serious food shortage, some Salzburgers even starving to death. By 1817, the population of only 11,000 was at its very lowest, and the following year a devastating fire reduced to ashes almost the entire district on the right-hand bank of the Salzach.[5]

This turbulent yet oppressive period also affected the ownership of the breweries. Most of the town's breweries changed hands within a short time. The actual structure changed little until the 1860s, and the number of breweries in the town remained constant at 13 – still manually operated establishments in small premises in the town's cramped space, producing between 2,000 and 5,000 hectolitres per year. The Province's only high-output brewery was that in Kaltenhausen, with an annual production of some 20,000 hectolitres.

The Getreidegasse showing the Sternbräu after 1900; on the right, the entrance to the brewery yard (now outdoor restaurant) with a poster advertising a concert. The façade advertises the *garden restaurant*.

The Sternbräu in the Biedermeier and Wilhelminian periods

Neither did time deal kindly with the Sternbräu, which changed hands every few years. Mathias und Anna Waldherr had been the owners since 1810, and after the death of Mathias Waldherr in 1822, his widow continued to run the business for ten years, until she died on 7 May 1832. The heirs, who had evidently no interest in keeping it going, decided to put the property to auction. The Sternbräu was valued at 13,700 gulden, and the date of auction was fixed for 22 October 1832.[6] Various appurtenances were offered separately for sale: *3 horses, one calèche, two small chaises, several carts, horse-gear, various items of jewellery and silver, garments and undergarments, several*

Inscription on the gravestone of the Stern brewer Mathias Schüssling (1815–1874) in St. Sebastian's cemetery in Salzburg.

items of linen, buckram, burlap, household, bed and table linens, pewter tableware, furniture, bedding and feather-beds, barrels with iron and wooden hoops, hand-tools and a number of books.[7] Disposing of the brewery and the inn, however, was apparently no simple matter. Not until March 1833 was the Sternbräu purchased by Michl and Barbara Wimmer, for a sum only 50 gulden more than the valuation price. Only three months later, the property was taken over by Josef and Barbara Hörl. Seven years later, in March 1840, the Sternbräu changed hands yet again; the new owners were Mathias and Cäcilia Schüssling (or Schiessling).

At this point, the neighbouring *Mödlhamerbräu* (Getreidegasse 26, now *McDonald's*) was also owned by members of the Schüssling family. They did not, however, run the Sternbräu themselves, but leased it to one Georg Ellinger.[8] From 1854, the Hörl family once again owned the Sternbräu – first Anton Hörl, and after his death in 1862 his widow Maria Hörl, who kept the business until 1885.

Little of note is reported of the Sternbräu until the 1850s. It was probably just an ordinary brewery with an ordinary inn serving an average beer, probably with mainly local residents as customers. The modest Biedermeier-period tourism, an excellent source of revenue for some sections of the Salzburg hospitality industry, passed by the Sternbräu. Contemporary travel reports, in which many other hostelries figure, make no mention of it at all.[9] The Sternbräu was not even a favourite haunt of the artists who flocked to Salzburg for its "mediaeval" ambience. Between 1815 and 1830, only eight names are registered of artists who put up at the *Goldener Stern* on their travels (of a total of 586 registrations in all the town's inns).[10]

The *Goldener Stern* did, however, have a hall which was suitable for festivities and was also used by travelling showmen and artistes for their performances. Here are

Poster announcing a *grand scientific art display* in the Sternbräu in January 1830.

Excerpt from the reference and address book of F. X. Weilmeyr, 1813, with a list of messengers waiting for clients in the Sternbräu.

two examples of entertainment popular in this period. In February 1825, the newspaper announced *a curious living society of Indian Bushmen from New Holland*.[11] The Bushmen were required merely to allow themselves to be exhibited; interested Salzburgers willing to pay 6, 12 or 24 kreutzer could attend the presentation of this *curious living society* in the Sternbräu hall and gape at the *Bushmen*.

A poster preserved since 1830 announces a *grand scientific art display* in the Sternbräu.[12] The illustration shows a figure lying in an open coffin, with lightning flashing down and a trumpeting angel above. In the text, one Sebastian v. Schwannenfeld declares that on 30 January 1830 he will have the honour of presenting his display for the last time, and therefore recommends it to the gentry, the military and the art-loving public. Viewers would be *surprised in the most striking way by physical-optic art products – never before to be seen here*. The venue was the *Sternbräu-Saale*;[13] seats cost – as for the "Bushmen" – 6,

12 or 24 kreutzer. Regrettably, the poster gives no indication of what was actually shown at the presentation.

Like other hostelries, the Sternbräu served as a stopping-off place for messengers who accepted letters and packages for delivery. It was the port of call for messengers going to Kirchberg, Kitzbühel, Lofer, Mauerkirchen, Tittmoning and Mühldorf. The messenger for Kirchberg and Kitzbühel, for instance, *arrives on Tuesday evening and leaves again on Thursday at midday;*[14] the one for Mauerkirchen *arrives every fortnight on Friday morning and leaves at 3 o'clock that same afternoon, lodging at the Sternbräu.*[15]

In the mid-19th century, the overall Sternbräu complex occupied a similar area to that of the present day, but was far more densely built than it is now. The building at Getreidegasse 34–36 housed the public bar, public rooms, hall, kitchen and living-quarters. The private chapel was in an annexe.

On the site of today's large self-service garden restaurant stood a two-storey building which housed the malting, brewhouse, fermenting and storage cellars. The brewhouse was on the ground floor, in a room with cross-vaulting supported by two central pillars. Until 1931, the Sternbräu's only traditional beer-garden was the small area now enclosed by arcades. Until the mid-19th century it had been surrounded by stables built partly of wood. The house at Griesgasse 23 also belonged to the Sternbräu complex, but at that time was not yet in use as a restaurant.

Anton Hörl (who purchased the Sternbräu early in 1854) and his successors carried out a whole series of constructional alterations. In 1858, for instance, the former stables – a long building which closed off the garden restaurant towards the Griesgasse – was adapted for catering purposes.[16] In 1862, Hörl embarked on modernisation of the technical production facilities *by installing an English double malt kiln in his brewhouse.*[17] In a malt kiln, the germinating or "green" grain is heat-dried to stop the germinating process so that it will keep. The new double malt kiln was installed in the first and second floors of the brewhouse; drying continued to be done in two stages – first on the higher level ("rack") at a moderate temperature, then after a few hours on the lower rack at a high temperature.

Anton Hörl died that same year, and the property passed in December 1862 to his widow Maria Hörl. Only six months later, further reconstruction was carried out – once again in the former stables along the side of the garden restaurant.

A plan of the site, dating from 1885, shows the building density of the Sternbräu site in the 19th century; the Getreidegasse runs along the lower edge, along the upper the Griesgasse, with an exit into it; the dark area shows the built-up Sternbräu complex, the light areas are courtyards, and – on the left, with the long building – the restaurant garden. The red rectangle marks a planned malting-house.

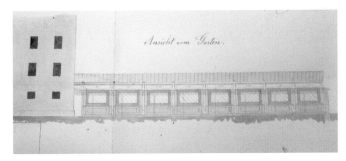

Plan for a veranda which stood in the (small) garden from 1864 until 1930/31, when it was replaced by the existing arcade.

The alterations *included a bar with closet on the ground floor, a staircase with a passage, and on the first floor a bar with closet*[18] and two public rooms. 1864 saw an interesting innovation: an old stall was demolished to make room for a long wooden veranda (29 x 3.6m) on the side facing the Getreidegasse. This remained until the renovations in 1930/31.

In a description of the brewery and its garden restaurant, a report from this period has little praise for the courtyard (the present large outdoor restaurant): *Tomorrow at about 11 o'clock I shall take you to the Stern Brewery in the Getreidegasse, provided that your nose will not be offended when we pass by the large stalls in the courtyards and unadulterated ammonia tingles in our nostrils.*[19] The verdict on the garden restaurant itself is somewhat milder, although the writer deplores the large number of customers: *You will be surprised to find it all so full of people already, although it is still rather cool and not yet midday, so that neither oppressive heat nor the sweat of long toil nor yet a salty dinner drives the thirsty hordes to the spring. I am merely taking the liberty of drawing to your notice the fact that this place – called a garden – has been restored (opened on Whit-Saturday 1864) and the salon is quite new.*[20]

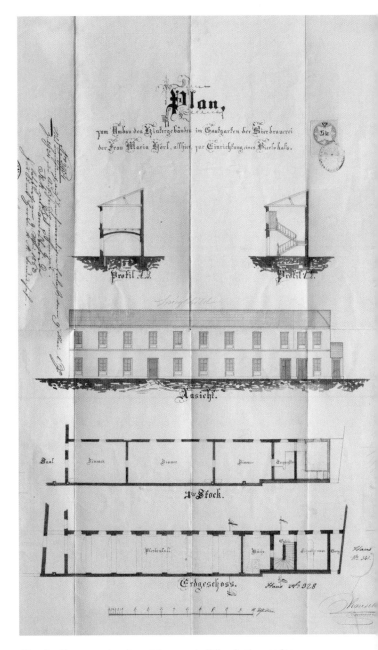

Plan for the reconstruction of the rear building in the garden restaurant of Frau Maria Hörl, brewer's widow, for the installation of a beer tavern. The plan, dated 9 May 1863, is kept in the Salzburg town archives. Today, the *Bürgersaal* stands on the site mentioned.

Invitation to a bowling match in the *newly-built Budl-Kugelstatt* in the Sternbräu, lasting from 8 May until 19 June 1865.

Invitation to a meeting of the *Allgemeiner Krankenunterstützungsverein* in the Sternbräu on 8 December 1871.

worked as a brewer in the Sternbräu. When they married on 12 August 1864, Maria Hörl was aged 36, Johann Schwaiger only 21. Although brewery and restaurant remained the property of Maria Hörl, Johann Schwaiger was ostensibly the "boss"; he continued as the *Stern brewer* and was responsible for running the Sternbräu until 1886.

Several posters have survived from that period, advertising various events held in the Sternbräu: one announces a bowling match lasting over 40 days, another the auction of a horse and several carts in the outdoor area, and yet another a meeting of the *Allgemeiner Krankenunterstützungsverein* [sick-benefits society] in the meeting-place of the *Arbeiter-Bildungs-Verein* [workers' educational association] (Sternbräu).[21]

Two major investments in particular were made during Schwaiger's management: in 1876 the beer-storage cellar was moved to the Riedenburg, at the foot of the Rainberg, and in 1885 the malt kiln was modernised once more.

As was customary at the time, the widowed Maria Hörl sought to secure and carry on the business by remarrying. She eventually found a new partner in Johann Schwaiger from Mühldorf in Bavaria, who probably

Rise and fall of the competitors

The second half of the 19th century was a period of far-reaching change for the town's brewing industry.[22] There had been hardly any developments in the breweries since the 17th century, but now events came thick and fast. General technical progress did not stop short of the brewing industry; the steam engine, larger premises for brewing and storage, ice-houses, bottom-fermented brewing, iron refrigerator ships, the introduction of the saccharometer, rail transport and finally the invention of the refrigerator revolutionised the entire sector. The Salzburg brewers were faced with the momentous decision between closing down, muddling through with a minimum of modernisation, or investing in modernisation and expansion, even building a new brewery on a different site. There were many reasons for closing down. Perhaps the brewery owner could find no successor, he had no capital to invest, he was in debt, or he might receive compensation from one of the larger modern breweries, which would purchase the brewery, immediately close it down and take over the customer base for its own business. In 1870 there were only nine breweries left in the town, producing a total of 44,467 hectolitres of beer.

Between 1848 and 1870 four breweries had already closed, and by the turn of the century the *Mödlhamerbräu* in the Getreidegasse, the *Schlambräu* in the Dreifaltigkeitsgasse, the *Bergerbräu* in the Linzergasse and the *Kasererbräu* in the Kaigasse had all closed down. From 1871, through partial modernisation and by moving the production premises (fermenting cellar, storage and ice-house) to what is now Hellbrunner Strasse 13, the *Höllbräu* in the Judengasse managed to keep the business going until it finally had to close in 1922.

Initially, only two breweries – Stiegl and Gabler – carried out comprehensive modernisation and expansion by moving to a larger site in the town. For reasons of production technology, Josef Schreiner, the Stiegl owner at the time, was the first to decide, in 1863, to move the brewery out of the cramped town premises to the more rural area of Riedenburg-Maxglan, where it remains to this day. Some years later, the *Gablerbräu* in the Linzergasse followed suit; in 1888/89, owner Franz Mayr had a new brewery built at the end of the Schallmooser Hauptstrasse (where the "Zentrum im Berg" now stands). The old *Gablerbräu* in the Linzer Gasse was gradually transformed into a hotel and restaurant. The only brewery business in the town to remain where it was, modernising its technology in 1911/12, was the *Augustinerbräu* in Mülln.

Beer production of the Salzburg town breweries in 1870	
Brewery	**Production 1870**
Stieglbräu	14.543 hl
Bergerbräu	5.766 hl
Sternbräu	4.629 hl
Gablerbräu	4.188 hl
Kasererbräu	4.120 hl
Mödlhamerbräu	3.509 hl
Höllbräu	3.197 hl
Schlambräu	2.648 hl
Mülln monastery	1.867 hl
Total	44.467 hl

Source: Statistical report by the Salzburg Chamber of Trade and Commerce to the Ministry of Trade, on production and transport conditions according to the results of the year 1870, Salzburg 1872, p 127.

From Sternbräu to Sternbräu AG [plc]

The further development of the Sternbräu is to be considered in this context. We do not know exactly why

Johann Schwaiger sold it in 1886. On 29 January of the previous year, Maria Schwaiger (formerly Hörl) had made over the entire property to her husband[23] – possibly due to her advanced age or to some illness. Johann Schwaiger intended to modernise the malt kiln again immediately, as an existing plan shows,[24] but it is not clear whether this intention was implemented. On 5 July 1886, the newspaper suddenly reported: *We learn from a reliable source that the large Sternbräu brewery in Salzburg has been purchased for the sum of 600,000 marks by Messrs. Felix and Max Wieninger in Reichenhall, J. Fromm in Augsburg, F. Angermann in Munich and the Spängler Bank in Salzburg.*[25] What could have been the reason for this sudden sale? Here we have only suppositions to go on. There may have been family reasons – the death of Maria, and no heirs to carry on the business (both daughters had married outside brewery circles and lived in Ried im Innkreis). Moreover, a definite role would have been played by the considerable purchase price, which guaranteed Schwaiger a secure livelihood for the future. In the contract of sale, dated 25 June 1886, the members of the purchasing group appear as: Max Josef Wieninger (brewery owner in Teisendorf, 1842–1910), Alwin Angermann (brewery owner in Hof/Bavaria, 1846–1929), Jakob Fromm (probably of the Joachim Fromm firm

of hop dealers in Augsburg and Munich), and Heinrich Ludwig Lochmann (details unknown). Within a year, the business was converted into a public limited company, with the declared aim of *the continuance of the beer brewery in Salzburg hitherto in the possession of Herr Johann Schwaiger in Salzburg.*[26] The principal of 250,000 gulden was divided into 1,250 shares of 200 gulden each. In May 1887, the business was entered in the land register as Sternbräu AG, and remained under this name until it was taken over by the Österreichische Brau AG in 1929.

As a public limited company, the Sternbräu was restructured to comply with modern requirements. There was now no longer a single *Bräu* [brewer] who was head of brewery and restaurant; instead, there was a managing committee, a board of directors, a brewery director and a restaurant manager. During the initial years, the managing committee consisted of Felix Wieninger (*d* 1904) and Ambros Passer (1860–1926). Felix Wieninger, a cousin of Max Josef Wieninger, was administrator of the *Fischerbräu* in Reichenhall. After Felix Wieninger's death, Dr. Otto Spängler was appointed to the committee in his place. Otto Spängler (1841–1919) was a cousin of Carl Spängler (1825–1902), founder of the bank of that name. Otto Spängler, too, was closely associated with Salzburg's commercial life. From 1876 until 1902 he was director of the Salzburg Sparkasse [savings bank] and intermittently vice-president of the local Salzkammergut railway, as well as chairman of the Achthal iron trade union (near Teisen-

Dr. Otto Spängler (1841–1919), cousin of the bank's founder Carl Spängler, played an important role in the commercial life of Salzburg; 1904–1919 he was president of the Sternbräu AG.

dorf in Bavaria).[27] Spängler remained a member of the Sternbräu AG managing committee until his death in November 1919. The brewery director from 1888 until 1926 was Ambros Passer from Ternitz in Lower Austria.

The first tenant landlord of the Sternbräu restaurant, from 1887 until 1894, was Franz Mayr. (It is not clear whether he was a member of the family that owned the *Gablerbräu*.) His successor for the ensuing ten years was Anton Brenner from Hypolz in Lower Austria (now part of the borough of Gross-Gerung), who had previously worked as head waiter in the Hotel *Stein*. In 1905 Brenner

Employment law provisions in the Sternbräu (1888)

The 1888 *work regulations for the Sternbräu brewery company in Salzburg*[28] offer an interesting insight into the late-19th-century world of work. Such regulations – which had to be made accessible to all employees, and to be openly displayed in businesses with more than 20 workers – were based on a change made in trading regulations in 1885, designed to provide better protection for factory workers. Until then, the working day for men, women and children could be up to 16 hours. In 1885, night-work and child labour were restricted, and the maximum working day limited to eleven hours.[29]

So what did this mean for the Sternbrauerei workers? Irrespective of their specific jobs, they were organised into six operational areas: brewers, coopers, engine- and boilermen, draymen, masons and carpenters, and wage-workers. The normal working day was eleven hours. For the employees in the fermenting cellar, storage cellar and coopery, the shift was from 5 a.m. to 6 p.m.; in the brewhouse, the working hours were calculated according to the brewing time (1 brew = 11 working hours); in the malthouse, work was round the clock, hours being divided so that *no more than 11 working hours shall fall within 24 hours.*[30] Breaks were allowed for breakfast, luncheon and afternoon snack, and according to the regulations, every worker was *entitled to take advantage of the 3 breaks.*[31] Thus the weekly working hours (Monday–Saturday) were limited to 66. Notice could be given by both employer and employee from one day to the next. Every brewery worker was required to join the *Allgemeine Arbeiter-Krankenkasse* [workers' health insurance scheme] in Salzburg, so that they were all insured against sickness and accident.

There was, however, still a long way to go before today's 40-hour week was reached. In December 1918 the 48-hour week was set by law, from 1959 it was the 45-hour week, and the 40-hour week was finally introduced in 1975.

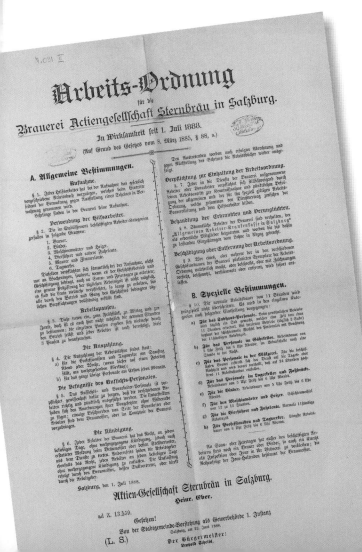

1l beer-stein from the Sternbräu with the monogram cut into the stoneware, c 1900.

was replaced by Karl Menzel (*b* 1875 in Vienna), who had previously been a waiter in the St. Peter Stiftskeller [monastery cellar restaurant]. Menzel remained tenant landlord until around 1914.

The competition never sleeps

The general demise of the breweries continued unabated until 1914. Of the 13 breweries remaining in the town in 1860, only five were left in 1912.[32] During the same period, the number of breweries in the whole crownland of Salzburg shrank from 75 to 36. Modern technology and new brewery buildings meant that fewer and fewer breweries were producing more and more beer. The larger breweries had little interest in the survival of the small ones, but certainly had an eye on their customer base. In 1912, the Stieglbrauerei and the Hofbräu Kaltenhausen brewed more than half the beer produced in town and Province together; the rest was divided between the remaining 34 breweries.

Since the beginning of the 20th century, Stiegl and Kaltenhausen had kept virtually neck and neck, with an annual production of some 100,000 hectolitres. Selling this quantity necessitated not only taking over the customer base of closing breweries and expanding along the railway routes, but also enticing customers in the catering business away from the competition. This led to fierce rivalry between the two largest breweries in the Province, which lasted until 1907. In the course of this unrestrained contention, not only did the rivals continually try to undercut each other, selling beer at sometimes completely unrealistic dumping prices, but also rewarding willing landlords with quantities of beer as benefit in kind. In order to increase their own customer base and reduce that of the rival, Stiegl and Kaltenhausen even went as far as taking over the debts of landlords who agreed to become their customers.

The breweries were not concerned exclusively with quantity, however – they also tried to attract the custom of prestigious catering establishments. On the other hand, they did their best to wall off their sales areas from large breweries outside the Province, such as Göss, Schwechat or Zipf, as well as those from Bohemia. The situation in Salzburg is, however, only a local example of the cutthroat competition in the overall beer market around the turn of the century. In 1895, Austria (today's borders) still had 543 breweries; by 1912 the number had shrunk to 289.

Beer production 1911/12	
Salzburg town	
Brewery	**Production in hl**
Stieglbrauerei	108,129
Sternbräu	*c* 35,000
Höllbräu	*c* 16,000
Gablerbräu	*c* 12,000
Augustinerbräu	10,500
Salzburg town total	***c* 181,629**
Salzburg Province	
Brewery	**Production in hl**
Kaltenhausen	136,000
Other 29 Breweries	139,772
Province of Salzburg total	**275,772**

Relocation: beer production moves to the Riedenburg

The Sternbrauerei was determined not to go under in this predatory competition. Since its purchase by the consortium and the conversion to a public limited company, beer production had almost doubled within a few years, from some 18,000 hectolitres in 1887 to around 30,000 hectolitres in 1895. During the ensuing years, the production remained stable – the brewery in the Old Town did not have the capacity for growth. The obvious idea, then, was to move the production premises out of the Old Town and build a new brewery. A site in the Riedenburg district at the foot of the Rainberg presented itself. The plot of land by what is now the Steinbruchstrasse had already been purchased in 1876 by the previous Sternbräu owners Maria and Johann Schwaiger, who had a storage cellar built there. The further development of this property, however, took place in instalments. For almost 20 years, the beer storage cellar was the only building on this land; there were no catering premises, as many other beer cellars in the town had. Not until the 1890s did a plan emerge to run a tavern beside the storage cellar, due to increased building and population in the inner Riedenburg district. From about the mid-1880s, a residential area grew systematically around the newly-built Neutorstrasse, with many villa-style multi-party houses.[33] As the population increased, the Sternbräu's arguments gained cogency. Its licence application in July 1892 reads to the effect that *the Bucklreith area has already become a quite presentable suburb of the town of Salzburg,*[34] and that many residents had moved into the new buildings.[35] Moreover, there had been many requests *to serve beer from our storage cellar.*[36] Since it was customary at the time to take a jug to the inn to fetch beer for drinking at home, they argued that the residents could not be expected to walk a long way to the nearest inn or tavern, *because the quality of the beer suffers considerably through being carried for a long time on hot summer days.*[37] The ensuing protracted discussion with the authorities over granting a licence went as far as the Supreme Administrative Court. Not until 1897 was agreement reached with the town that no new licence would be granted, but an already existing one transferred.

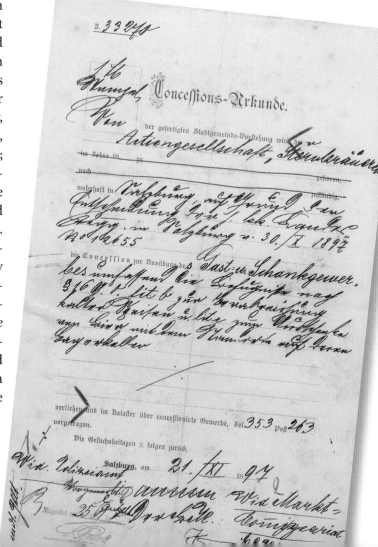

Licence to serve alcohol to the public in the storage cellar of the Sternbräu in the Riedenburg district, issued on 30 October 1897.

The Sternbrauerei in the Riedenburg after completion, view towards the Mönchsberg and the Neutor.

In November 1897, authorisation to serve beer at Siegmundsplatz 5 was transferred to the storage cellar of the Sternbrauerei, and the pub was opened under the name of *Sternkeller*. Three years later, the licence was extended to allow hot food to be served. The frequent change of lessee indicates that the business did not run quite smoothly: between 1897 and 1909 alone, the pub had five different landlords. It was not until Martin Bruckbauer took it over in 1909, and later Alois Schnöll, that a period of continuity settled in, and lasted for decades.

Efforts by the Sternbrauerei to move production to the Riedenburg dragged on for six years. Many local residents fought tooth and nail against the construction of a large brewery, exhausting all legal channels. This time it was protesting residents who took their objections to the Supreme Administrative Court. In brief, events followed thus: an initial plan for moving the production from the Getreidegasse to the Riedenburg dated from 1900. Several residents appealed against the positive decision by the mu-

nicipality in August 1900, first of all to the town council, then to the Provincial government (the Court of Appeal, as trade authority). The latter refused permission to build the brewery, whereupon the Sternbräu AG lodged a ministerial appeal, which also met with a refusal in January 1902.[38] Thus the first round of the dispute was decided in favour of the local residents.

In August 1902 the Sternbräu AG launched a second attempt, submitting to the town council a new, improved project with a 56m-high chimney. This project was once again approved, partly because *no danger or nuisance is occasioned to the neighbourhood, since on the one hand modern technical experience does in fact allow smoke-free combustion, and on the other the disposition of the chimney, according to its planned situation and height, also appears adequate for preventing any nuisance to the surrounding area through smoke or soot.*[39] The local residents promptly objected to this positive decision, and it was in fact repealed by the Provincial government which, while admitting that the new project showed considerable improvements in the avoidance of smoke and soot, pointed out that things looked different *if this complex is to be built in a narrow valley basin closed on 3 sides, as the Riedenburg is, if such a large industrial concern is to be established in the middle of a villa quarter – which, like the Riedenburg, as a select residential area requires increased hygienic protection.*[40] Concerns included smoke-logging, smoke as a hygiene hazard, adverse effects on the development of the district and depreciation of the existing buildings. Once again, the Sternbräu AG lodged a ministerial appeal – this time successfully: with an order dated 17 June 1903, the

Entrance to the Sternbräu from the Griesgasse, *c* 1900. Today's large open-air restaurant is still completely built up.

ACTIEN-GESELLSCHAFT STERNBRÄU SALZBURG.

The Sternbrauerei in the Riedenburg, in a 1914 edition of the daily newspaper *Salzburger Chronik*.

Haus Wawra, Wien, VIII., Wickenburggasse 14.

Gruß aus dem Sternbräu (Salzburg).

Restaurant garden *c* 1910/12; background left: the staircase to the "Gartensalon"; right: the entrance to the *Altdeutsche Stube* (now the *Bürgersaal*).

July 1907, the new brewery was at last completed. Contractor and probably also planner was the Salzburg architect and master builder Jakob Ceconi.[44] The press rejoiced at the new brewery. The *Salzburger Volksblatt* wrote: *Salzburg can definitely welcome the valuable addition of such a fine, exemplary establishment,*[45] and the *Salzburger Tagblatt* expressed delight *that the entire complex is equipped with the most up-to-date brewing technology*, allowing the Sternbrauerei *to double its production, which has hitherto been in the region of 35,000 hectolitres per year.*[46] This never happened, but the general feeling was one of optimism.

Inn and garden in the "glorious beer years"

In the three decades prior to 1914, spacious beer gardens were all the rage in Salzburg – giving breweries and restaurants the convivial "beery" ambience typical of this period, as described in travel guides and the feuilletons of major newspapers. Figuring prominently was the atmosphere in the *Müllner Bräustübl* and the *Stieglkeller*. Other popular beer gardens in and around the Old Town were the *Schanzlkelle*r (Schanzlgasse 14, now Landeskindergarten) and the *Electrischer Aufzug* restaurant on the Mönchsberg (on the site of the Museum of Modern Art). The Sternbräu beer garden fitted perfectly into this list. The Sterngarten was the only beer garden right in the Old Town, as well as dating back to the 18th century and possibly even earlier. In reports about the Sternbräu, the

Ministry of the Interior countermanded the decision of the Provincial government. The opponents of the project now had final recourse to the Supreme Administrative Court which, however, rejected the appeal, the verdict of 5 April 1905 finding it *partly unfounded, partly inadmissible.*[41]

Thus the way to building the new brewery was clear. The ground-breaking ceremony took place on 25 June 1906, and construction took little more than a year. The *Salzburger Tagblatt* paid tribute to the progress in lofty terms: *Today saw the completion of the mighty 58m-high chimney, towering above the Rainberg – a prodigious structure, the equal of which is to be found nowhere in the whole land.*[42] It continues: *Day by day, hundreds of passers-by followed the gradual soaring of this mighty yet not unshapely colossus, whose profane purpose it is to protect from any smoke nuisance the Riedenburg residents, who have now, one and all, come to terms with the new brewery complex.*[43] In early

Poster (March 1898) advertising the limited sale of "Salvator-Bier".

Poster (March 1904). "Salvator-Bier" had been re-named "Josefi-Bier".

public rooms in the building at Getreidegasse 34–36 are hardly mentioned, but only the restaurant garden and the rooms adjoining it. Access was possible from both the Getreidegasse and the Griesgasse.

Around 1900, the outdoor area consisted of the tree-planted garden, closed on one side by the long, narrow wooden veranda. Towards the Griesgasse, the garden was bordered by a two-storey outbuilding with public rooms: on the ground floor an *altdeutsche Stube* [old-German-style room] and a *Bräustübl* [beer bar]; on the first floor the *Gartensalon*. Sometimes there was a bowling alley in front of this outbuilding.

Sternbräu advertisement in the travel guide *Salzburg und Umgebung* (1897).

Gasthof und Garten-Restaurant „Sternbräu" Salzburg. Karl Menzel.

Restaurant garden *c* 1910/12 towards the Bader- and Sterngässchen. Foreground left: the new veranda built in 1910; visible behind it is the long veranda of 1864. The outhouse on the right is now the site of the *Bürgersaal*.

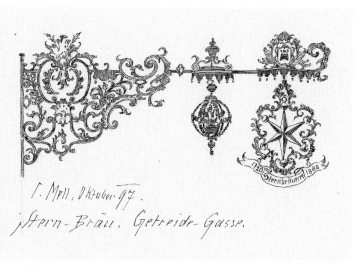

The Sternbräu sign in the Getreidegasse, ink drawing by Karl Mell, 1897.

The newly-established Sternbräu *AG* evidently took great pains to refurbish the inn. At the beginning of 1888, for instance, the distinctive Sternbräu sign hanging in the Getreidegasse was given a completely new look; it was re-hung on 18 February amid celebrations, for which restorer Franz Mayr engaged the *Concert-Kapelle Schneider*, which played for the *festive inauguration*.[47]

The more interesting and spectacular event, however, was the start-up of the electric lighting installation in the Sterngarten[48] on 16 May 1888. At this time, the use of electricity was still in its infancy. By the end of 1887 there were only 60 customers with around 500 light bulbs in Salzburg; two years later 2,38 lights bulbs were in operation. So the electric lighting in the Sterngarten was something special. The opening was accompanied by a *concert with the entire regimental band*.[49] The garden was filled to capacity, and the public *delighted by the magnificent light illuminating the garden, making it as bright as day*.[50] The *Salzburger Zeitung* congratulated the brewery on this innovation, *which will be an exceptional attraction for visitors*.[51]

We learn from a contemporary source that even before the turn of the century the problem of space in both the garden and the public rooms had become acute. To quote from a poem recited on 16 March on the occasion of broaching the first barrel of *Stern-Salvator* beer:

Wie wär's, wenn da die Bräuerei –
Es wär' ja wirklich nichts dabei –
Bald bauen würde ein Lokal
Für fünf-, sechshundert an der Zahl

Die Bräuerei wird's nicht geniren,
Sie würde doch nur profitiren;
Hier mitten in der Stadt nun gar
Würd' mehren sich der Gäste Schar.

Gut wär' gesorgt für Frau'n und Herrn,
Bei unserm lieben gold'nen Stern! –
Der Herr Verwalter wär' der Mann,
Der so etwas durchsetzen kann.[52]

[*Imagine, if the brewery –*
this isn't just a reverie –
were soon to build a fine beer-hall
for five, six hundred overall.

The brewery would not regret,
expenses it would soon offset;
here, in the centre of the town,
the crowds would flock and bring renown.

"Fine fare for all" is the concern
of our belovèd Gold'ner Stern! –
The Herr Direktor has the skill
to bend conditions to his will.]

The *Herr Verwalter (Direktor)* refers to brewery director Ambros Passer, mentioned elsewhere in the poem as a member of a card-playing clique that had been playing *Vierer-Schnapser* [four-handed 66] in the window-corner to the left of the door for over twenty years.

Wer sich einmal dorthin verirrt,
Der wird sofort auch expedirt.
Gleich heißt's mit Zorne im Gemisch:
„Das ist der Schnapser-Extratisch!"[53]

[*Should one mistakenly approach,*
he's set upon with prompt reproach
and driven thence with angry words:
"This table's ours for playing cards!"]

A further detail from everyday life in 1899 is revealed: to the annoyance of customers, the entrances to the Sternbräu, both from the Griesgasse and from the Getreidegasse, seem to be frequently obstructed by vehicles.

Der Eingang von der Griesgass'-Seite
Bereitet uns nicht immer Freude,
Weil oft ein Wagen da, sammt Pferd,
Uns diesen Eingang halb versperrt.

Kommt man von der Getreidegass',
Da ist's auch oftmals gar kein Spass,
Man muss da gehen kreuz und quer
Und find't den Eingang wirklich
schwer.[54]

[*The entrance from the Griesgass' side*
is not always a source of pride,
for often there's a horse and dray
blocking half the entrance-way.

Getreidegasse's much the same –
to enter here's no simple game,
you have to weave your way around –
the entrance isn't easily found.]

So the last resort was often to enter from the Bader- or Sterngässchen:

So bleibt der Zutritt noch von hinten,
Den aber Fremde nicht leicht finden.[55]

[*There's still the entrance at the rear,*
but strangers won't find their way here.]

The "Stern-Salvator" beer was re-named "Josefi beer" some years later. This was a bock beer served annually in mid-March (*for a short time only*),[56] and was *so popular with the public that every year supplies ran out far too soon.*[57] Broaching was celebrated every year with great to-do. The costumed figure of King Gambrinus would enter, to the strains of a wind band. Available all year round were *our widely acknowledged prime light (Pilsner type) and dark (Bavarian type) beers, with a flawless flavour.*[58]

Poster with calendar for 1909. In the foreground is a drinking scene, the people in Biedermeier attire; in the background, a costumed group approaches with King Gambrinus on a beer barrel.

Around the turn of the century, there was extreme rivalry between the local breweries, as well as with breweries over the border. Thus the Sternbrauerei urged customers: *So forget all prejudices and drink our local beer!*[59]

The memoirs of Berta Köckerannerl (1882–1953) allow us an insight into the everyday life of the Sternbräu around the turn of the century. Berta, who probably worked in the bar or the kitchen, describes how she broke the personal beer-mug belonging to Herr Leopoldsberger, a regular customer: *The mug broke, it was a china mug, the pewter lid remained. There was a lot of shouting and commotion, but the mishap had already befallen. I promised to replace said mug, and that I would apologise to Herr Leopoldsberger was a matter of course. The next day I came, all sheepish, and begged pardon. But he took my hand and said: "But why are you so worried, that could just as well have happened to me, and I'll get another one – it wasn't all that valuable anyway."*[60] Two years after this incident, Köckerannerl married regional poet and writer Otto Pflanzl, who was a beer salesman for the Stieglbrauerei.

Now that the tourist industry was really taking off, the Sternbräu aimed to attract not only local residents, but also the "foreigners", the tourists. The travel guide *Salzburg und Umgebung* (1897) includes the following notice: *Sternbräu garden Getreidegasse in the town centre. Old German-style beer bar, well worth a visit. Widely acknowledged best beer in Salzburg from our own brewery, and excellent Viennese cuisine, with friendly service and low prices. Guest rooms available. – Lovely shady garden.*[61] Similarly in the catalogue *Salzburg, Stadt und Land*, published in 1902 by the Landesverband für Fremdenverkehr [regional tourist association]: *Old-established brewery and inn (founded in 1542). – Situated in the town centre, with a large, shady garden. – Widely acknowledged excellent beer. – Viennese cuisine. – Very reasonable prices. – Attentive service.*[62]

Very tempting – let's go!

In 1910, further investment was made in the garden, with a second wooden veranda, to be seen on various postcards from this period. It was built in place of the ice-house, which was no longer necessary since the storage cellar, fermenting cellar and brewery were moved to the Riedenburg. A small bandstand, built earlier, was used by bands and groups of musicians, as in the summer of 1910 by the *Sänger- und Musiker-Gesellschaft Familie Kamberger*, who performed at 8 p.m. every Tuesday and Wednesday, their highlight being *"The World's Smallest Schuhplattler"*. World famous![63]

Shortly before the outbreak of World War I, a further major change took place in Salzburg's brewing sector. In 1913 the Sternbräu AG bought up the Gablerbrauerei. The *Gablerbräu* – at this point the oldest still existing brewery in Salzburg, had been owned since 1868 by the Mayrs, a well-known Salzburg catering family. After Franz Mayr's death his sons and heirs, Franz and Fritz, sold the "Gabler" to the Sternbräu AG. This brought the number of traditional Salzburg breweries down to four (Stern, Stiegl, Höllbräu and Augustinerbräu Mülln). A newcomer since 1901 was Adalbert Behr's Weissbierbrauerei. The *Gablerbräu* had been brewing some 12,000 hectolitres of beer annually; now this quantity was taken over by the Sternbräu which, with its new brewery in the Riedenburg, was well equipped to cope with a greater capacity. The business prospects looked good, and the company was confident. The developments from 1914 onwards, however, caused this optimism to fade, and the trend was soon reversed.

Clearing the way for traffic: 20th-century breakthrough fantasies

From the beginning of the 20th century, the "modern age" entailed frequent "regulation plans". These involved broad, straight routes through the Old Town, which would necessitate demolishing old building fabric and erecting new "better-looking", more functional buildings. One of those unrealised projects concerned a road tunnel through the Mönchsberg from the Kapitelplatz to Nonntal. This would have wiped out most of St. Peter's cemetery. A further plan, proposing a breakthrough from today's Herbert von Karajan Platz to the Griesgasse, kept reappearing at intervals between 1908 and 1928, and five variations were worked out in detail.[64]

While Josef Schubauer's 1908 breakthrough project would have entailed demolishing the *Mödlhamerbräu* (Getreidegasse 26), Franz Wagner's plans would have had a disastrous effect on the Sternbräu: the planned road would have run from the Neutor via the Karajanplatz and the area of the demolished *Goldener Hirsch* hotel, across

Plan of a road project from the
Griesgasse towards the Neutor (1908).

DURCHBRUCH ZUM NEUTORTUNNEL · M.1:1250

NORD

Plan of a (fictitious) road project from 1933: it shows the breach
through the houses in the Old Town from the Neutor to the Salzach.
The Sternbräu complex and other buildings would have had to make
way for it.

the Getreidegasse, and *through a large arcaded courtyard (Sternbräuhof)*[65] to the Griesgasse. Little would have remained of the Sternbräu itself. This very project raised its ugly head one last time in 1933, in a dissertation by Martin Cäsar at the Technical Academy in Vienna.[66]

In view of the steadily increasing traffic, Cäsar's thesis planned a car-friendly town, but paid little heed to established structures. Cäsar adapted Franz Wagner's plan, and drew up a direct route through the old buildings. The

projected road would run straight through the historic Sterngarten and the high school (now AVA Hof), emerging into the Franz Josef Kai a short distance downriver of the *Makartsteg* [footbridge].

The only breakthrough to be implemented here was in 1953: the so-called "Griesgasse breakthrough" owes its existence to the massive destruction caused by Allied bombing during World War II.

Advertising sign for Sternbräu beer, 1920s.

Uncertain times: war and post-war years

The beginning of World War I saw a drastic change in the lives of the Salzburg population. The initial euphoria soon faded away, as people readjusted to war economy. Food and raw materials were rationed, food ration cards introduced, and the general deterioration of the supply situation meant that every household and every business was affected. 1915 was already completely dominated by the development of the war economy.[1] April 1915 saw the introduction of the bread and flour ration card, with which one could buy either 28 decagrammes [≈10 ounces] of bread or 20 decagrammes [≈7 ounces] of flour at one of the 25 issuing offices in the town. A month later, there were two meatless days a week, and soon ration cards were distributed for diced bread [for making traditional dumplings], sugar, milk, soap and potatoes.[2] The last two war years in particular were marked by food rationing, requisitioning, hunger and shortage economy.

The breweries were of course badly affected by the shortage of raw materials. February 1915 saw the founding of the state "war grain transport organisation", which had a monopoly to purchase grain directly from the producers to store as a central reserve, and to distribute it at fixed prices.[3] So the breweries could buy malting barley only through this organisation. The allocated quantities of barley were distributed by the Brewing Industry Association and the Society of Malt Manufacturers. In 1917 and 1918, the breweries in the Austrian part of the empire received only a meagre 3% of the amount they required in peacetime. Towards the end of the war, the only available beer

was produced from substitute ingredients. Whereas in 1913/14, the last year of peace, the crownland of Salzburg had brewed more than 450,000 hectolitres of beer, the brewing year 1917/18 produced the scant total of 75,000 hectolitres. Similarly in the Sternbrauerei, where the 1913/14 production of 43,000 hectolitres was reduced to just under 7,900 hectolitres in 1917/18. As early as December 1914, the brewery complained about the conscription of *well-trained, efficient workers*, as well as the constantly rising prices of all requisites. The company's board of directors found the prospects for the years ahead less than encouraging: *In such critical times, when all values are fluctuating, it is always a difficult matter to draw up a balance-sheet equidistant between optimism and pessimism.*[4] In February 1915 a blanket prohibition was issued against malting barley. The Sternbrauerei was obliged to hand over 30% of its barley and malt reserves to the "war grain transport organisation". In 1916, the brewery could purchase neither barley nor malt. Sugar was used instead of malt for brewing, until the sugar reserves were also confiscated. Things became even worse, however. In order to brew something that remotely resembled peace-time beer, from 1917 *pure ersatz ingredients were used*[5] – but these, too were finally confiscated. Little remained of the convivial pre-war beer culture. The *Stieglkeller* had been closed since 1916, a war kitchen was set up in the Sternbräu, and *tall grass runs riot in the Bräustübl garden!*[6] According to the "Ruperti Kalender", the small quantity of beer allocated to inns and restaurants was exhausted within minutes. This, it stated, had wrought changes in the physical constitution of the town's residents: *Formerly portly*

Salzburger Kriegsküchen. Heute um 10 Uhr vormittags fand im Sterngarten die Eröffnung der vom Konsumentenverein geschaffenen Kriegsküchen zur Erleichterung der Nahrungssorgen der Minderbemittelten statt. Unter den Anwesenden waren u. a. Landespräsident Dr. v. Schmitt-Gasteiger mit Hofrat Hiller und Landesregierungsrat Rambousek, Exzellenz Graf Kuenburg mit den Mitgliedern des Kriegshilfskomitees, Stationskommandant Oberst Brocien Dembicki, Etappen-Bezirkskommandant Oberst von Ternowsky mit mehreren Offizieren, Landesausschuß Daniel Etter und Landeskonzipist Dr. Mehrl für den Landesausschuß, Bürgermeister Ott, Gemeinderat Beinkofer und mehrere Gemeinderäte, Direktor Passer für die Sternbräuerei und Regierungsrat Spängler, für die Stiglbrauerei, sowie sämtliche Damen des rührigen Damenkomitees. Der Obmann des Hilfsvereines für Konsumenteninteressen Dr. Mussoni schilderte nach kurzer Begrüßung der Gäste die Entstehung der Kriegsküchen und verwies auf die mitwirkenden Faktoren, wie Staat, Land, Gemeinde und Aktiengesellschaften. Schließlich betonte er die Notwendigkeit des wirtschaftlichen Durchhaltens zu dem alles zusammenwirken müssen. Landespräsident Dr. v. Schmitt-Gasteiger sprach Worte der Anerkennung für die Leistungen des Hilfsvereines und sicherte dem Institute seine weitere Förderung zu. Regierungsrat Spängler erwiderte auf die anerkennenden Worte der beiden Vorredner für die Brauereien und versicherte, daß es ihnen eine Freude sein werde, auch fürderhin nach Kräften die Bestrebungen zu fördern, die den Minderbemittelten die Existenzmöglichkeit in der schweren Zeit schaffen. Hierauf folgte die Besichtigung der Räume, deren zweckmäßige Einrichtung vollen Beifall fand. Besonderes Interesse erweckte die Kriegsküche selbst, deren Öfen von den Titaniawerken in Wels geliefert worden sind. Mögen die Kriegsküchen den Minderbemittelten und Armen der Stadt eine Erleichterung in den Nahrungssorgen bringen und in allen Kreisen jene Förderung erhalten, die sie verdienen.

Zur Kundenanweisung. Parteien, welche noch keine Anmeldezettel zugestellt erhalten haben, wollen unverzüglich solche bei der städt. Kanzleidirektion Rathaus 1. Stock abholen und ausgefüllt dortselbst oder bei einer Sicherheitswachstube abgeben. Es ist dies im...

Newspaper article in the *Salzburger Chronik* of 15 November 1916, concerning the opening of a so-called war kitchen in the Sternbräu.

Announcement in the *Salzburger Chronik* of 1 April 1917, that the municipality was to take over the war kitchen in the Sternbräu, with immediate effect.

townsmen have been transformed into svelte figures; beer bellies and beer hearts have become clinical rarities.[7]

In provisioning the population, an important part was played by the communal kitchens which were set up, some as early as late summer 1914. As the war continued, many such canteen kitchens were installed in order to ensure a more efficient use of food resources – the recipients carefully separated according to social groups. This gradually gave rise to emergency kitchens (for the unemployed and destitute), war kitchens (for the "indigent"), and so-called "middle-class" kitchens.[8]

The first war kitchen in Salzburg was opened on 15 November 1916 in the garden wing of the Sternbräu. From then on, if not before, the beer garden and adjoining premises were closed to ordinary visitors, while the rooms at Getreidegasse 34–36 remained open. All local dignitaries, from the Provincial president downwards, were

Kundmachung

betreffend die Uebernahme der Kriegsküche durch die Stadtgemeinde.

Mit **1. April 1917** wird im Sinne des Kriegsküchen-Erlasses die Kriegsküche in der Sternbrauerei (Getreidegasse) in den Betrieb der Stadtgemeinde übernommen. Eine durchgreifende Neuorganisation des Betriebes wird in der nächsten Zeit vorgenommen werden. Vorderhand werden ab **Sonntag, den 1. April** folgende Anordnungen getroffen:

1. Infolge Mangels an Lebensmitteln und wegen Ueberbürdung des Personales **entfällt die Abgabe der Abendmahlzeit.**

2. Bis zur Neuregelung des Preises für den Mittagstisch wird nur eine **einheitliche Mittagskost** zum Einheitspreise von 60 Heller verabreicht.

3. Um eine rationelle Ausnützung der Vorräte zu ermöglichen, wird eine Mahlzeit nur denjenigen Personen verabreicht, welche sich **bis spätestens 2 Uhr nachmittags des Vortages in der Kriegsküche (Sternbräu) gemeldet** und den hiefür entfallenden **Betrag eingezahlt** haben. ◆ Die Kassastunden werden von 9 Uhr vormittags bis 2 Uhr nachmittags festgesetzt. Für die Mittagsmahlzeit am Montag, den 2. April 1917, hat somit die Anmeldung und Einzahlung bereits Sonntag, den 1. April, bis 2 Uhr nachmittags zu erfolgen.

Stadtgemeinde-Vorstehung Salzburg
am 31. März 1917.

present at the inauguration of the war kitchen, and praised the "benevolent society for consumer interests", which acted as sponsor. The official speeches were followed by *the visitation of the premises, the functional appointments of which were greeted with unanimous applause. Of particular interest was the war kitchen itself, where the ovens were supplied by the Titania factory in Wels.*[9] The declared purpose of the war kitchen was *to provide a good, nourishing midday meal and a simple supper.*[10] The menu offered *⅜ litre soup and ½ litre vegetables with an addition (blood-sausage, polenta slices, dumplings, etc.)* for 60 heller, or *⅜ litre soup and about 30 decagr. dessert*[11] for 40 heller. The supper also consisted of ⅜ litre soup and an open sandwich, for 24 heller. In addition, a warm breakfast was provided daily for 1,000 needy schoolchildren, either served directly in the Sternbräu or delivered to the schools in hay-boxes. Whole crowds of people flocked to eat in the war kitchen; between 15 November and 31 December 1916, more than 7,000 midday meals were served. In March 1917 alone, this number had risen to over 51,000 midday meals – a daily average of 1,645.

On 1 April 1917 the municipality took over the war kitchen in the Sternbräu. From December the war kitchen also served as a so-called "Abendheim" [lit. "evening home"] – a *Wärmestube* [lit. "warm room"] for people living in unheated homes or rooms. They could spend the evening there from 5 until 8.30 p.m. with no obligation to consume food or drink.[12] The increasingly dismal supply situation led not only to resignation and passive resistance, but also to "poverty crime" of theft and burglary. The Sternbräu frequently had to report thefts. Leather driving-belts were a favourite item among stolen goods; no less than three times, the Sternbräu *AG* reported burglaries with the loss of more than 20 metres of such belts.[13] Even the war kitchen had unwelcome nocturnal visitors who stole food and shoes.[14] There was occasional bill-dodging, and clothing was stolen from the public room.

The final months of the war were marked by complete inner disintegration. The supply situation among the population was catastrophic. From 11 August 1918, *the serving of any kind of meat, or any dishes containing meat, [was] prohibited in all commercial catering establishments (hotels, restaurants, soup-kitchens, etc. etc.) in the town of Salzburg.*[15] This injunction, issued initially for one week, was repeatedly extended. From 18 August 1918, there were severe restrictions on serving food to strangers in restaurants; for instance, strangers were permitted to eat only in the hostelry where they were staying overnight. Local residents with *ration cards for persons entitled to board at a hostelry*[16] were to be given precedence over strangers. Anyone visiting Salzburg without an overnight stay could collect a "food pass" at the town police station for one meal only. *Therefore catering establishments offering no accommodation are permitted to serve food of any kind only to local residents or to strangers who show and hand over such a food pass.*[17] However, these and similar measures brought no relief to the food situation. People ate turnips and used bran instead of flour; burnt acorns were ground to make coffee powder, and bread was made with corn-meal ("polenta bread"). Finally, hunger drove thousands on to Salzburg's streets. In the "hunger demonstration" of 19 September 1918, women, soldiers and Russian prisoners of war, in unwonted concord, marched through the town, plundering as they went.[18]

Shortly before the end of the war the Sternbräu separated brewery and restaurant: the Sternbräu AG sold the original building in the Old Town and restricted its activities to the production premises in the Riedenburg. This step is explained by the wretched circumstances during the war years. The press reported the sale of the old Sternbräu building *including the garden and outbuilding on 26 July 1918;*[19] the contract of sale was signed in September 1918. The purchasers were, with equal shares, Friedrich and Maria Schiller, who ran an alcohol-free

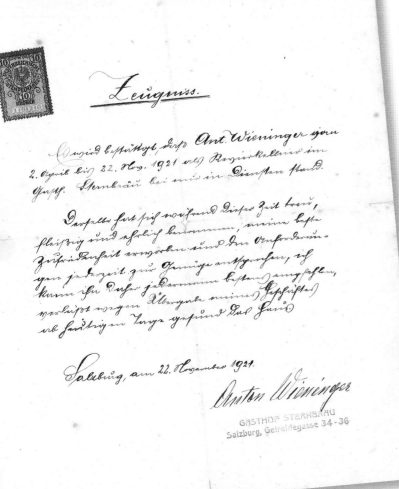

Testimonial for the chef de rang Anton Wieninger jr., drawn up on 22 November 1921 by his father Anton Wieninger sr., who was until then manager of the Sternbräu.

bräu went to the hotelier, litérateur and bon-vivant Alois Grasmayr (1876–1955)[22], who owned the *Stein* and *Bristol* hotels and the *Blaue Gans* restaurant.

Until 1925 the owners were Grasmayr and Maria Schiller, with Anton Wieninger employed as manager until the end of November 1921. The Sternbräu, like the eating-house in the Dreifaltigkeitsgasse, was probably run for a time as an alcohol-free restaurant. In a letter from the *Stadtbauamt* [municipal planning and building control office] it was clearly termed an *alcohol-free eating-house*[23] – an interesting development, considering its original function. It was probably not until 1923, when Karl Kranzinger took over the Sternbräu as tenant landlord, that beer was once again served there.

Although several breweries had tried to start up again after the end of the war, between 1912 and 1923 the number of breweries in the Province had decreased from 36 to 22. In the town, the *Höllbräu* closed its brewery in 1922, leaving only three established breweries: Stern, Stiegl and Augustinerbräu Mülln. The Weissbierbrauerei in Schallmoos had existed since 1901. The Sternbrauerei made great efforts to come gradually closer to the pre-war production figures, but tax increases and the rising cost of raw materials meant constantly raising the price of beer, which in turn led to a reduction in sales – or such was the opinion of the Sternbräu AG board of directors. There was nevertheless a cautious optimism, because *wine has become considerably more expensive and the small quantity of apple cider imported ought to have a favourable influence on beer consumption.*[24]

During the first post-war years, the worst shortage in the breweries was that of coal. In the spring of 1920 Franz Rehrl, then still deputy Provincial governor, interceded in

eating-house in the Dreifaltigkeitsgasse, in the former Lodron Primogeniture Palace (now the façade of the Mozarteum University). The newspaper mentioned the purchase price as 200,000 kronen,[20] while the Sternbräu *AG*, taking into account the total inventory, gave it as 620,000 kronen.[21] In April 1920, a half share of the Stern-

View of the street façade of the Sternbrauerei in the Riedenburg during the inter-war period.

"Sternbier" barrel-filling during the inter-war period.

this matter with the competent state secretary in Vienna, Johann Zerdik, who promised to allocate ten tons of coal each *to the breweries "STERNBRÄU" and "STIEGL" in Salzburg*.[25] Rehrl expressed polite thanks for the allocation, but in his reply he requested Zerdik *to render possible a larger delivery to the aforesaid breweries, since 10 tons of coal for one month would probably be rather too little*.[26] We do not know how the matter ended; only a month after Rehrl's reply, Zerdik was replaced as state secretary.

"D'Kreuzlschreiber" folk theatre society

In the course of its history, the wing of the Sternbräu which adjoins the old (small) restaurant garden, and which now houses the *Bürgersaal*, has had many different functions. Originally used as stabling for horses, it retained this function until 1858. Since then it had been used only for catering purposes. In the years prior to World War I, there was a so-called *altdeutsche Stube* [old-German-style room] on the ground floor, and on the first floor a *Gartensalon*; sometimes a bowling alley was set up in front of the building.

The *altdeutsche Stube* was replaced for over two years by an amateur theatre, where from October 1923 until the end of 1925 performances of *folk plays with professional actors excluded* were given,[27] organised by the Salzburg folk theatre society "D'Kreuzlschreiber", founded in 1919. Very little is known about this society; on the committee

were Erich Schmuck and Otto Grantner. The name was presumably taken from the title of the folk comedy by Ludwig Anzengruber. In the autumn of 1923, the long, narrow room was converted into a theatre; the auditorium – some 20 metres long and 5.5 metres wide – was licensed to seat 110 spectators sitting at tables, as for variety theatre. About two months after the series of shows began, there was an official inspection, which found many deficiencies – including the lack of spittoons. The theatre society justified this failing by asserting that *there were currently none to be had in Salzburg*.[28]

Before their first performance, theatre productions which had not yet been shown in Salzburg were subject to *the special approval of the Provincial governor*.[29] The plays selected were fairly innocuous, intended purely to entertain. In autumn 1923, for instance, the plays included *Almenrausch und Edelweiss* and *Die Herrgottsbrücke*.[30] By the end of 1925 or spring 1926, performances in the Sternbräu came to an end. The major renovation in 1926 left no room for the Thespians. We do not know how or whether the society continued.

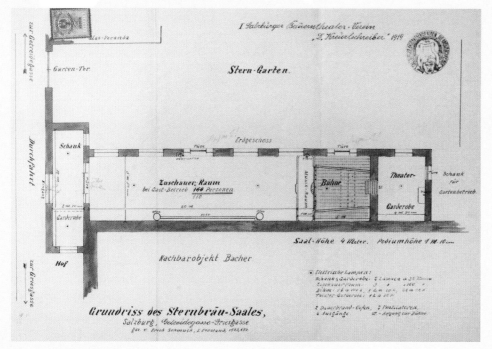

Plan of stage and auditorium of the theatre society "D'Kreuzlschreiber", drawn in 1923. Until at least 1914, this was the site of the *altdeutsche Stube*; today it houses the *Bürgersaal*.

The "golden twenties"
of the Salzburg catering industry

With the introduction of the schilling currency in 1925 and the end of inflation, the catering industry regained its optimism. From the mid-1920s onwards, a remarkable will to investment was evident in many hospitality businesses, restaurants, coffee-houses and cafés, triggering a wave of modernisation and expansion.[31] Most of the conversion and new building was carried out during the years 1925-1928, in the hope of economic upswing, increasing tourism and political stability.

One of the most striking developments in the catering industry, and one that altered the historic townscape, was the building of the *Stieglkeller* below the Fortress. In 1925, the flagship of the Salzburg beer-hall, which had reopened only in 1922, became a major construction site, reopening once again in May 1926. The *Müllner Bräu*, too, expanded during this period. Although it already had two large halls to accommodate the thirsty population, this was evidently insufficient. 1925/26 brought hall no. 3, designed (like the two existing halls) by Salzburg architect Karl Pirich (1875–1956). In the *Pitter* hotel, the *Pitterkeller* was redesigned and moved to a new site in 1926. The press deemed the new premises, with room for 550, as *practical and with a homy ambience.*[32] A year later, the restaurant of the *Zipfer Bierhaus* on the Universitätsplatz was renovated, to designs by the sculptor Jakob Adlhart (1898–1985) and the later National Socialist architect Otto Strohmayr (1900–1945). Some of the furniture (*heavy, massive tables, ready to offer the hard-drinking carouser an agreeable place to be*)[33] is still there. Also in 1927, the *Traube* hotel and its restaurant (*famed for its food*)[34] in the Linzer Gasse was

Notification from the municipality of Salzburg, dated 23 February 1925, to the effect that with the re-acquisition of the Sternbräu complex by the Sternbräu AG, the licence granted to the premises is transferred to the new owner.

renovated, and in the same year the *Münchnerhof* hotel, restaurant and wine bar was completely reconstructed. The business that succeeded the old *Schlambräu* in the Dreifaltigkeitsgasse and Lederergasse was completely gutted and refurnished according to latest standards. Conversions and additions were carried out in the *Meran* hotel in the Plainstrasse, the *Bristol* on the Makartplatz, the inns *Zum Hirschen* in the St. Julien Strasse, *Zum schwarzen Rössl* in the Bergstrasse, and the *Tiger* in the Linzer Gasse, *which is in the process of setting up a new beer bar with a distinctive entrance.*[35]

1925/1926: New owners, reconstruction and extension I

Since 1922, the bookseller Adolf Stierle had been president of the board of directors of the Sternbräu AG. As such, he endeavoured to re-acquire the Sternbräu inn as

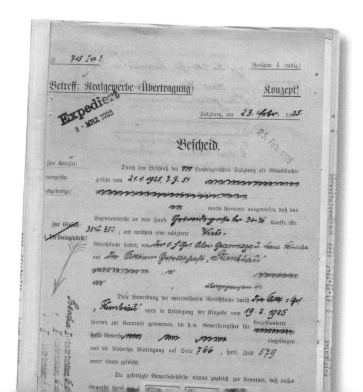

part of the company. Finally, at the beginning of 1925 the Sternbräu AG managed to purchase the business again.[36]

The next step was total renovation of the entire premises – twice in quick succession, in the space of six years. In 1926 and again in 1930/31, the building complex between Getreidegasse and Griesgasse was one huge construction site. When the finishing touches had been put, and the Sternbräu was opened at the beginning of May 1931, Salzburg had a completely refurbished, state-of-the-art catering establishment which remained substantially unchanged over the ensuing decades.

First of all, the company had been concerned with *renovating the completely neglected premises, which demanded much work and large sums of money*.[37] The next move soon followed: on 28 December 1925 – again on the initiative of Adolf Stierle – the Sternbräu AG purchased the adjoining house, Griesgasse 25.

Advertisements in the *Salzburger Chronik* and the *Salzburger Volksblatt* announce the re-opening of the Sternbräu after reconstruction, to take place on 23 September 1926.

Restaurant *Zur grossen Tabakspfeife* or *Bacherscher Glassalon* at Griesgasse 25. The salon was converted into the Sternbräu dining-room in 1925/26.

This house belonged to the Bacher family, who had also run an eating-house there since the 1870s – most recently named *Bacherscher Glassalon* or *Restaurant zur grossen Tabakspfeife* – which consisted of a bar and a dining-room. A few months later, alterations were carried out to join the two sites, making the Sternbräu into one large inn. The building permit is dated 3 March 1926. The premises adjoining the garden opened in May, and finally the restaurant as a whole on 23 September 1926. It was in this first reconstruction phase that the floor plan took the form that remained essentially until 2012. The *Bacherscher Glassalon* became the Sternbräu dining-room, *welcoming and hospitable*, and the new public rooms facing the Griesgasse *are no less characterised by tasteful comfort*.[38] Today's *Bürgersaal* was on its present site, though at that time it was called the *Gartensaal*. Great pride was taken in the *ultramodern kitchen premises, probably unique in Salzburg*.[39]

The opening of the new Sternbräu was announced in large newspaper advertisements which promised *completely re-furnished rooms and beer bars*, not forgetting to mention that people *were welcome to bring their own food*.[40] The original rooms at Getreidegasse 34–36 were still open, and were now known as *Sternbierhallen*. After all the renovation and extension, however, the all-year-round operation of the Sternbräu moved towards the Griesgasse.

A new Sternbräu landmark appeared on the roof of Griesgasse 23: the *electric lighting system*,[41] visible from afar. Salzburg's very first neon sign of this size was of course not greeted with unadulterated enthusiasm, but regarded extremely critically in various quarters. The town council expressed a negative view of the advertisement, criticising *the unfavourable effect of the neon sign mounted on the roof* and demanding *within 14 days of receipt of this decree, a sketch of an altered version with a precise descrip-*

tion.[42] According to the description, the original version was a star in a bluish-purple ring, star and lettering being *extremely blurred and wellnigh unrecognisable*.[43]

The Sternbräu AG thereupon had a modified neon sign made and mounted on the roof in 1927. This new landmark, consisting of *1 large star, with a diameter of 2.50 metres from point to point, with blue neon light, under it the word "Bräu" with letters 1m high in red neon light*,[44] still shines out into the night, as the oldest existing neon advertisement in the town of Salzburg.

In the course of the renovation, an old wrought-iron inn-sign was mounted on the façade of the building at Griesgasse 23; it had originally shown a medallion with the town's coat of arms and a leaf medallion with the figure of an angel. The conjecture is that it was a wall-bracket on

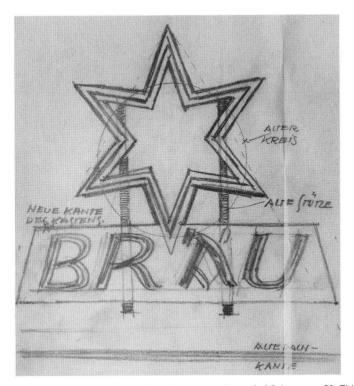 

Pencil sketch for the neon advertisement on the roof of Griesgasse 23. This version was eventually implemented.

The old wall-bracket of the *Stadttrinkstube* became the Sternbräu sign in 1927; here it is shown, freshly renovated, in 2014.

the former *Stadttrinkstube* on the Waagplatz, which arrived here by a devious route.[45] The angel was replaced with a star; the sign *staged a colourful come-back and now adorns the Griesgasse.*[46] Freshly refurbished, after the 2013/14 reconstruction it is displayed in the same place.

The new lessees of the of the reconstructed Sternbräu were Markus (1872–1933) and Aloisia Wagner (1873–1944). Markus Wagner can be seen as a typical representative of the landlord generation of the time: having no public house of their own, he and his wife leased a new business every few years. Thus – like many of their colleagues – they made the rounds of the town's catering businesses. From around 1899 until 1904, Wagner was tenant of the *Weisser Adler* at Bergstrasse 14, until 1918 he was manager of the *Deutscher Hof* (Hubert Sattler Gasse 12, now the *Vier Jahreszeiten* hotel); then he managed the *Stieglmayer* inn (later *Weinhaus Moser* at Wiener Philhar-

Aloisia Wagner (seated 3rd from right) with the kitchen staff.

monikergasse 3), and finally in 1926 he took over the Sternbräu for four years.

He recommended his restaurant in the following terms: *Newly renovated and extended, with verandas, glazed room, dining-room and beer bars … Tasty Viennese cuisine à la carte and table d'hôte. Alternating concerts. Landlord Markus Wagner guarantees sound management and prices.*[47] Or this: *First-rate Viennese cuisine, well-matured beer, light and dark, from our own old-established Stern-brauerei (founded in 1720), natural wines. Reasonable prices. Alternating concerts. Restaurateur Markus Wagner extends a cordial invitation to patrons.*[48] (The year 1720 – still to be seen on the Sternbräu wall-bracket in the Getreidegasse – probably refers to the birth year of *Stern* brewer Johann Mathias Wilhelmseder.) After his period as Sternbräu lessee, Wagner purchased the *Guggenthaler Bierstübel* at Linzer Gasse 20, and was at last his own master. He died soon after, in 1933, but the building and the business remained in his family until 1971.

Today it is the *Stadtkrug* hotel.

The kitchen staff at the Sternbräu under the management of Markus Wagner (on the left with his wife).

Menu cover, c 1927/28. The drawing shows the corpulent landlord.

Gaſthof
Sternbräu
Sterngarten
Salzburg
Telephon 440

Pächter Markus Wagner

Allfällige Beſchwerden bitte direkt bei dem Pächter vorzubringen

Entwurf: Markus Wagner jun.
Druck: Funder & Müller, Salzburg

Karl Reisenbichler's paintings

In 1929, the artist Karl Reisenbichler received a commission for several oil paintings with motifs from Salzburg's history, to hang in the so-called *Gartensaal* of the Sternbräu. Within only a few weeks (so it is said) Reisenbichler painted no fewer than eleven pictures, which were *handed over to the public*[49] on 16 August 1929. Ever since then, the pictures have graced the room now known as the *Bürgersaal*, still hanging in their original place after the major 2013/14 reconstruction. They show the Salzburg Archbishops Leonhard von Keutschach, Matthäus Lang von Wellenburg and Wolf Dietrich von Raitenau, the old Salzburg annual fair held on the Cathedral Square, four scenes from the Salzburg Peasants' War, the burning of a witch, traders on their way over the Radstädter Tauern pass, and the flight and capture of Archbishop Wolf Dietrich von Raitenau. The sombre paintings with their predominantly serious subjects lend a distinctive ambience to this room.

There is a persistent rumour that Reisenbichler painted the pictures merely *in return for board and lodging*.[50] This was probably not so, for during this period the artist received a number of commissions in Salzburg. Apart from the works mentioned, there are pictures that Reisenbichler painted at the behest of the Mattighofen brewery, for the *Platzlkeller* which opened in 1927.

Karl Reisenbichler (*b* 2 March 1885 in Attersee/Upper Austria) trained in Vienna as an "academic painter" from around 1902 until 1908, and was a member of the *Salzburg Kunstverein* from at least 1913. After the First World War, *still painting in the spirit of the Secession and Expressionism, with a tendency towards social and rural pathos, he was also inclined towards the art that is close to nature and the people.*[51] Staunchly German-national in his political views, Reisenbichler became more and more of a sympathiser with National Socialism. Finally, he moved to Munich as an "illegal", returning around 1938 to Salzburg, where he was appointed to the regional management of the Reich Chamber of Culture (Fine Arts). After 1945 Reisenbichler lived in reduced circumstances in Grossgmain, where he died on 21 December 1962.[52]

Karl Reisenbichler, traders on their way over the Radstädter Tauern.

Several of his works are still on display in public space in Salzburg. From 1927, he executed sgraffito works on various house façades, including the "Thalhammer-Haus" at the corner of Getreidegasse/Sigmund-Haffner-Gasse, Denkstein shoe shop (formerly Café Lohr) at the corner of Linzer Gasse/Dreifaltigkeitsgasse, "Ankerhaus" on the Waagplatz (former *Stadttrinkstube*), and the former Bacher bakery in the Willibald Hauthaler Strasse. Other works have disappeared, such as that on the façade of the house at Platzl 5, which was demolished, and the works on the façades of the "officers' houses" in the Reichenhallerstrasse, through heat insulation measures. The pictures in the workshops in the former Kiesel printing works are damaged, and stored temporarily in a school.

Karl Reisenbichler, Archbishop Wolf Dietrich von Raitenau.

1929–1931: New owners, reconstruction and extension II

One might have supposed that after the 1926 renovation the Sternbräu was now completely up to date, and that everything would settle down peacefully. Sometimes, however, "the best-laid schemes" soon turn out contrary to expectations. A further change in ownership structure created completely new requirements. In June 1929, an inconspicuous single-column report in the *Salzburger Volksblatt*, under the heading "Volkswirtschaft" [national economy], announced major innovations: *It has come to our notice that in recent days negotiations held between the Österreichische Brau-A.-G. and the Aktiengesellschaft Sternbräu in Salzburg concerning the take-over of the Salzburg brewery company by the Brau-A.-G. have reached conclusion.*[53] In the same edition is an advertisement placed by lessee Markus Wagner, with the same text as that in 1926

Loading ramp of the Sternbrauerei, 1930s.

Loading transport barrels at the ramp in the Sternbrauerei, 1930s. The man in the kalmuck jacket, keeping a written record, is presumably Sternbräu lessee Franz Kitlitschka.

Title page of an advertising booklet for the Sternbrauerei after the takeover by the Österreichische Brau AG, c 1931.

(see above). The entry in the land register was made on 15 April 1930, hardly a year later.[54]

With the takeover of the Sternbräu AG, the Österreichische Brau AG established itself in Salzburg for the first time. The company – already the largest brewing concern in Austria – had developed from the parent company "Braubank AG", founded in October 1921 and consisting of the following companies: Poschacher Brauerei in Linz AG, Wieselburger Aktienbrauerei formerly K. Bartenstein, Linzer Aktienbrauerei und Malzfabrik, Salzkammergut-Brauerei in Gmunden and the Brauerei Kaltenhausen near Hallein. The basic idea was to merge the breweries *for joint planning and equipment of the breweries and for joint purchasing, with the aim of standardised commercial management and elimination of the uneconomic competition between the five breweries.*[55] Four years later the full merger was accomplished and the name changed to "Österreich-ische Brau Aktiengesellschaft", Brau AG for short, indicating *that the "Braubank", founded as a parent company, had become a beer-brewing enterprise.*[56] In Austrian terms, this meant that a real beer empire had been created. It was soon responsible for 20% of Austrian beer production, constantly expanding by buying up further breweries. Adolf Stierle, until then president of the board of directors of the Sternbräu AG, was now given a seat on the board of directors of the Brau AG.

The Sternbrauerei in the Riedenburg continued to operate, at first producing almost 50,000 hectolitres per year. From the beginning of the 1930s, however, the economic crisis and unemployment reduced the production to less than half (in 1933/34 only 20,000 hl).[57]

The takeover by the Brau AG apparently entailed a demand for further building extension. In retrospect it was maintained that after the merger with Brau AG *the trans-*

Summer 1930: the restaurant garden with the Kitlitschka couple, the lessees (standing on the left) in the final year before the reconstruction. In the background is the wooden pavilion from 1910.

Demolition work in the Sternbräu courtyard, 1930/31. A simple, single-storey building then adjoined the arcades.

formation of the entire property into a modern licensed house in a manner similar to that of the large Munich breweries was decided.[58] According to the protocol of the building negotiations in February 1930, the plan was initially to build a cellar under the bar and the arcades along the garden, and to add an extra storey to part of the wing running along the passage between Griesgasse and Getreidegasse.[59] In the course of the year, however, ideas went more in the direction of a far more lavish restructuring. The dimensions of the building project grew increasingly comprehensive. Construction began after the summer season, in the autumn of 1930. *When work had begun on demolishing the old masonry according to the original plans by the architect*

The loggia room with illustrations by Theodor Kern. This was the trattoria *La Stella* from 1987 until 2012.

The restaurant garden with the arcades, built in 1931 and still in existence.

Franz Wagner jr., [they] recognised that it would make more sense to carry out the bulk of the work at one go.[60]

Thus the winter months of 1930/31 saw the largest construction site in the Old Town. In December 1930 the *Salzburger Chronik* reported that the Sternbräu building site was a point of interest for the whole town, and had become an attraction for the local population. *Every day, curious onlookers flock to see the demolition work.*[61] Within six months, the entire Sternbräu had been turned upside-down. Work was carried on day and night, in two eight-hour shifts, *which in the worst period of unemployment provided a welcome opportunity to earn money.*[62] Remarkably, during the whole reconstruction period, the restaurant was open as usual. This demanded a great deal from the

The *Bürgersaal* with the paintings by
Karl Reisenbichler has remained unchanged.

In today's *Braumeisterstube* beer bar, little has changed since 1926.

Newspaper announcement
of the re-opening on 2 May 1931.

lessees – since the end of 1929 the Kitlitschkas – and all the staff: *Only a professional will be able to appreciate fully just how much work and daily commotion the lessees Franz and Fanny Kitlitschka had to put up with during the alterations, in order to keep the business going.*[63]

The construction work, which went on until the end of April 1931, brought results both visible and invisible to the public. The old restaurant garden was now framed by arcades supported by marble pillars, and the glassed-in loggia room had been decorated by *the talented painter* Theodor Kern (1900–1969) with murals showing various tavern scenes.[64] (This was the trattoria *La Stella* from 1987 until 2012.) Added to the existing rooms on the ground floor were now the *Jagdzimmer*, and the *Ritterstüberl* as the meeting-room for the "Mauternburger Ritterschaft" [knights of Mauternburg]; on the first floor were six club-rooms.

The wing along the passage between Griesgasse and Getreidegasse was completely rebuilt, and the chapel it had housed (*the contents of which were taken to St. Peter's*) was demolished.[65] (All that re-

The Sternbräu wing between the large and small restaurant gardens, as it was between 1931 and 1986.

mains of the contents are two figures representing Saints Benedict and Rupert, exhibited in the DomQuartier since 2014.) Several utility rooms (including butchers' premises, cold-storage room, pump chamber, water supply and central heating rooms) had been installed in the cellar, and – not least – *telephone booths with automatic doors* in the foyer.[66]

The most conspicuous alteration was the demolition of the old brewery building, which had been closed down in 1907. It was replaced by the second (larger) *Stern* garden with eight high chestnut trees, bar and long benches *which, as a beer garden with self-service, where patrons were permitted to bring their own food, gave this part of the complex the desired character.*[67] Above the bar was a terrace in which, as the newspaper report feared, *probably sometimes a "Trudering-style" band will arouse mixed feelings among those present and in the neighbourhood.*[68] In view of the new rooms and space in the garden, the original public rooms and the public bar at Getreidegasse 34 were closed, bringing to an end a catering history going back over 400 years. Until 1986 there was to be hardly any change to this catering concept.

The new garden with young chestnut trees created around 1931, after the former brewery building was demolished.

Town council v lessee: the "piggery" case

Although this was prohibited, many citizens allowed their pigs, goats and cows to run free in the town and fed them in troughs placed in front of their houses.[69] This remark refers of course to mediaeval Salzburg – but centuries later, livestock was still kept within the town walls. Right into the 20th century, stables were not uncommon in the Old Town. However, the pigsty housed in one of the Sternbräu buildings until the end of 1930 was rather an exception. After the end of World War I, a former stable in the Sternbräu grounds, beside the passage to the Getreidegasse, was converted into a pigsty. In May 1921, the Salzburg building authority granted retroactive permission to keep pigs, although *strictly speaking, for reasons of hygiene a pigsty in the densely populated Getreidegasse would certainly not be tolerated …*[70] Permission was granted only *in consideration of the current particularly difficult food situation.*[71] For the ensuing ten years, there was no further mention of a pigsty. It was only in February 1930 that several neighbouring residents took action; they wrote a joint letter to the police complaining of what they considered the intolerable stench, expressing their desperate situation in graphic terms: the effluvia were *so nauseating that it is wellnigh impossible to remain in the house, since even when the windows are closed, they penetrate into the apartments and offices and pollute the air.*[72] They pointed out that now, in winter, the windows were mostly closed anyway, which clearly showed *the impact of this stench on the residents during the summer months, when they were obliged to keep the windows open.*[73] Moreover, the residents complained of *such a plague of flies that they were unable to fend them off, since there would be hundreds of flies in one room – which is anything but beneficial to health.*[74] The police reacted to this complaint with a letter to the town council, reporting that *according to police investigations, the account given in the letter of complaint was in accordance with the facts,*[75] and requesting the council to prohibit the keeping of pigs in the Old Town. The subsequent correspondence shows that Franz Kitlitschka, the lessee of the Sternbräu, was then forbidden to keep pigs. An inspection carried out by police officer Karl Walkner on 21 June 1930 revealed, however, that in the Sternbräu grounds not only were there 15 pigs, but in addition a completely new pigsty.[76] The police officer's report was immediately forwarded to the council, together with an urgent request *to arrange for the pigs to be removed as soon as possible.*[77] In a hearing on 12 August 1930 *on the premises at Griesgasse Nr. 25,*[78] it was agreed by a committee consisting of representatives of the town council and the police, lessee Franz Kitlitschka, and one representative each of owners and neighbouring residents, that the *pigs held without official authorisation were to be removed by 31 December 1930 and that henceforth no more pigs shall be kept in this building.*[79] Since the Österreichische Brau AG had long since drawn up the reconstruction plans for the Sternbräu grounds, this was more of a symbolic action. Building work began in the late autumn of 1930, and nothing more of the matter has been heard since.

Festival season – crisis season

Hardly had the Sternbräu re-emerged in 1931 as a large, completely refurbished restaurant, than the political and economic crises of the 1930s gave it a rough time. Within only a few years the world economic crisis, mass unemployment, expiry of insurance benefits, impoverishment, the transition from democracy to authoritarian corporative state, the attempted coup by the National Socialists and the so-called "thousand mark barrier" brought a whole series of catastrophes upon Salzburg.

For a start, the restaurant – now with two gardens, several public rooms, club rooms and a large dining-room – had to be run cost-effectively. The local customer segment consisted of individual guests, regular midday and evening guests, numerous clubs and societies, and organisers of social events (lectures, balls, etc.). Foreign guests had become rare. The ban on any political activity for the Austrian branch of the NSDAP was countered in 1933 by the German Nazi government with the "thousand mark barrier". From 1 June, German citizens wishing to enter Austria had first to pay 1,000 marks to the government at the relevant passport office. For tourism in Salzburg, this meant the loss of the German middle-class tourists. "Jupp from Wuppertal", the typical German "backpacker" *who used to be seen in droves, with his blue jacket, his binoculars hanging round his neck, his celluloid map-case and his alpenstock covered with badges, populating especially smaller boarding-houses, beer gardens and mid-range hostelries,*[80] had now vanished entirely.

The number of German guests staying overnight in the town of Salzburg dropped from 119,000 (32.5 % of total overnight stays) in the tourist year 1931/32 to 6,700 (2 %) in 1934/35.[81] The tourist deficit was just about balanced by well-to-do Festival visitors from other countries, who enjoyed the ambience of an authentic rustical inn.

The rapid reduction in beer production can be taken as an indicator of the economic situation. Whereas in the

The Getreidegasse with the historical Sternbräu wall-bracket and (in the foreground) a new light-box, probably 1930s.

Beer-mugs with the Sternbräu emblem, from the time between 1910 and 1940.

Invoice for beer, dated January 1935, to the *Gasthaus Spielberg* in Grödig.

Letter of complaint from Emil Ludwig, 1935.

brewing year 1929/30 410,000 hectolitres were produced in the eleven breweries in the town and the Province of Salzburg, within a few years production had dropped by almost half, and in 1933/34 it was only 232,000 hectolitres. This downward trend could also be observed in the production figures of the Sternbrauerei (1929/30 still 48,000 hl, in 1933/34 only 20,500 hl).

An invoice for beer, dated January 1935, to the *Gasthaus Spielberg* in Grödig gives an idea of the scant beer sales in the inn. In this generally low-turnover month, the inn purchased from the Sternbrauerei 170 litres of draught beer, (cost price 64 groschen per litre) and 175 bottles of beer (cost price 39 groschen per half-litre bottle). This is equivalent to a daily average of around eleven half-litres draught and six bottles.

A letter from Emil Ludwig, rector of a secondary school in Vienna, to Hans Hofmann-Montanus, director of the Salzburg tourist office, offers a little insight into the daily course of events in the 1935 summer season. Ludwig complains about a number of incidents in the Sternbräu.[82] We learn that the set midday menu cost 2.20 schillings in 1934 and in 1935 was increased to 2.60 schillings. Ludwig taught holiday courses for English teachers; every year he came to Salzburg for a week with the course participants, and *he had for many years dined together with them in the "Sternbräu" at midday and in the evening*; moreover, *the Sternbräu had become the regular meeting-point for convivial evening gatherings.*[83] The group consisted daily of between ten and fourteen persons.

The occasion of the letter was relatively trivial. The group had been served roast veal as the main dish at midday on three days running. When on the third day a lady in the group asked for the (cheaper) macaroni, she was told that either she had to take the set menu or pay the full amount for the macaroni. After an heated altercation between group, waiter, and landlord Franz Kitlitschka, the group moved with one accord to the *Höllbräu*, since they *had already been sufficiently annoyed by various instances of rudeness in the Sternbräu.*[84] We do not know how the matter ended; in any case, from 1936 the Sternbräu had a new landlord, Karl Ohneiser.

Nazi rule and war

At the beginning of 1938, social life in Salzburg carried on as usual. Gatherings and events were held in the Sternbräu as though in a peaceful age of economic prosperity with no political tensions. The Salzburger *Tierschutzverein* [society for the protection of animals] held its general meeting in the Sternbräu on 4 January (with chairman Bernhard Paumgartner (1887–1971), better known as composer, conductor and rector of the Mozarteum Academy), and discussed, among other things *the so-called pigeon question.*[85] On 16 January, the *Salzburger Freiwillige Rettungsgesellschaft* [voluntary rescue society] hosted a ball with the motto "Film night in Hollywood", and a few days later, amid stuffed animals, hunting trophies and *jolly, racy decorative paintings*, the Salzburg hunt held their "Hubertus ball", at which the guests *were soon in the most festive mood.*[86] A regular event in the Sternbräu was the *Faschingsgschnas* [carnival revel] of the "Typographia" male-voice choir, this year with the motto "Ball on Capri". Elaborate decorations, costumes and masks which *in surprisingly great number, looked really inventive*, made the ball, according to the

1938: German Wehrmacht marching through the Getreidegasse.

newspaper report, *one of the best in this carnival period.*[87] Not everyone who came was admitted: *But what did the few hundred have to say, who were refused entrance because the "Stern" was already crammed to bursting-point with some thousand Capri travellers?*[88]

On 11 March 1938, the German Wehrmacht entered Salzburg, and with it National Socialism – joyfully acclaimed by some, but for others the beginning of fear and terror. In fact, the National Socialist era in Salzburg began for many with a euphoric expectation that "everything would get better". When it ended, in the spring of 1945, people had to bring their own cutlery, salt and sugar to public houses.

At first the feeling of hope predominated. Many Salzburgers longed for the so-called Anschluss with the German Reich in March 1938 to put an end to the economic downswing, bringing instead work and earning-power. Linking Salzburg and Austria with the boom in the German arms industry, which in 1938 already accounted for 50% of German public expenditure, also fuelled the Austrian economy. Unemployment in both town and Province dropped from December 1937 to December 1938 from 23% to under 4%, which in turn stimulated consumption. Organised KdF tourism[89] brought masses of citizens from the Reich to spend holidays in Austria, which delighted especially the catering businesses and breweries. We have no production figures for the Sternbrauerei from this period.

Therese Spiegel, like many others, suffered fear, terror and finally murder. She owned an antiques business in the old Sternbräu house at Getreidegasse 34, which was plundered and destroyed in 1938 in the course of the November pogrom, by organised SA and SS raiding parties.[90] The *Salzburger Landeszeitung* reported that a *violent mob* was responsible for the destruction of Jewish-owned shops, and that *Spiegel's antiques shop also came to grief.*[91] Therese Spiegel and her husband were taken to the Theresienstadt concentration camp in 1942, and deported that same year to the Treblinka extermination camp, where they were murdered.[92]

Swedish tenor Set Svanholm (1904–1964), photographed on 20 July 1938 in the restaurant garden of the Sternbräu.

The Sternbräu inn was given the honorary title of "Kampflokal" because in the period of the corporative state it had (along with other inns) been a meeting-place for the illegal National Socialists,[93] – which was not surprising, since landlord Karl Ohneiser had declared himself a party member immediately after the Anschluss. Within the company, diction and terms were adapted to those used in the National Socialist ideology. The *Belegschaft* [personnel] became the *Gefolgschaft* [followers], *Brauereidirektor* Sepp Passer became *Betriebsführer* [works manager] Sepp Passer. The first *grossdeutsche Betriebsweihnacht* ["greater German" company christmas party] for the brewery staff in the Sternbräu dining-room affirmed the solidarity of the business as being like that of a large family, *where followers and works manager have formed a unit.*[94] A similar line was taken by the *Kreisleiter* [district leader] in his address: the Sternbrauerei was a company *in which the proper spirit of co-operation and solidarity existed between manager and followers.*[95] According to reporter L. A., several of the employees were so moved by this that they begged manager Passer to forget

115

The Bürgersaal during the NS era; a swastika flag hangs on the chandelier.

whatever might have(!) *stood between them at some previous time*.[96] And Passer? In his great joy at the *veritable peace celebration of this Christmas party for the company family*,[97] he was only too happy to make this promise. Then the brewery staff and their families were treated to a handsome bounty: on top of a Christmas gratuity and wage increase for those enlisted for military service, every employee received a Christmas gift of 50 marks, for pensioners and widows 15 marks, for every unprovided child or grandchild a parcel containing warm underwear and a bag of baked goods. Three weeks later, in the barrel-pitching hall of the brewery, the military band of the *Gebirgsjägerregiment* I/137 [mountain infantry] gave a concert which was broadcast on radio.

From then on, the events held in the Sternbräu served mostly the purposes of party and state. A convention of the Nazi Party Old Town local branch (*Pg.* [party member] *Klostermann from Gera gave an excellent and vivid account*

of the absolute logic and purposeful, systematic planning of all the measures taken by the Führer[98]) was followed by a meeting of "brain-injured war veterans" (the main task of war victim support was *to render the brain-injured front-line combatants once more fully operational*[99]) and a "Mutterkreuz" [Mother's Cross of Honour] award ceremony (*All those present listened, profoundly moved …*[100]).

One of the last major civilian events to be held in the Sternbräu was entitled *Die automatische Waschfrau* [the automatic washerwoman]. This was a presentation of *an automatic household washing-appliance*, which in a single operation *heats, washes, rinses and bleaches*.[101] In November 1939 the firm of Dal-Pont placed large-scale advertisements in the newspapers, promoting their latest household achievement: the washing machine. Between 20 and 29 November three demonstrations were held daily in the Sternbräu for interested housewives. *No-one should miss this major event*, for: *the automatic washerwoman is an unpar-*

alleled achievement of German technology! Ingeniously combined, simple construction! Top-quality material![102] The longer the war went on, the more acutely did scarcity make itself felt in everyday life. A visit to a public house entailed food stamps, "field kitchen dishes", small beer and ersatz ingredients. On 19 December 1942, Hitler Youth musicians from the Riedenburg local branch gave a performance in the Sternbräu, the proceeds of which went to the Winterhilfswerk [winter relief fund]. In this period there was already a marked labour shortage, and in the catering industry nearly all the employees were women. One fine Sunday in the summer of 1943, almost 2,300 people flocked to the Sternbräu. Unqualified staff consisting of 65 women and 5 men had to cope with this crowd of largely "impatient guests".[103] The landlord at this point was still Karl Ohneiser, who in 1941 was named "Gaststätten-Meister" [master landlord] and awarded the "master's pin". In spring 1944, however, he was suspected of "economic offences against war regulations", details of which are not known. The circumstances of his profession might suggest illegal slaughtering or manipulation of food stamps. At any rate, in May 1944 he was barred from running the Sternbräu. Allegedly, the Deutsche Arbeitsfront (DAF) [German Labour Front] hoped to use this episode to confiscate the Sternbräu for use as a soup kitchen. By immediately replacing him with a new lessee, it was possible to prevent confiscation, and business could be carried on.[104] The new lessees, who started work on 1 June 1944, were Alois and Anna Schnöll, who had until then managed the Sternkeller, the Sternbrauerei public house in the Riedenburg; they continued to run the Sternbräu until 1959.

In the autumn of 1944, Salzburg finally came under Allied air attack. From October 1944 until the beginning of May 1945 the US Air Force bombed the town in fifteen attacks, primarily with the aim of disrupting rail communications, and killing a total of 547 people. Off-target hits caused much collateral damage, including massive destruction in the Old Town. The Sternbräu was fortunate for quite some time and

December 1942: Hitler Youth band performs in the Sternbräu.

avoided substantial damage. However, just before the end of the war, on 25 April 1945, it was damaged in the penultimate attack. Starting at 10h58 that day, 109 B-24 bombers, called "Liberators", attacked the town, dropping 997 bombs. The station area, the district of Lehen, the Old Town and the area around the airport in Maxglan were all struck. In the Old Town, the area between St. Blasius' Church and the Sternbräu is in ruins.[105] Buildings totally destroyed included Getreidegasse 48 and 50, Badergässchen 1 and 3, Sterngässchen 6 and Griesgasse 25, this last being part of the extended Sternbräu since the 1926 reconstruction. Contemporary witness D. G.: The front of the Sternbräu was as normal, but at the back, half of it was missing – where you go into the hall today, from there half of it had been ripped away.[106] The intact parts of the restaurant nevertheless continued to operate. D. G. lived in the house next door and was bombed out; at a collection point she was given a wooden spoon, a wooden fork and a food voucher, which we had to take to the Sternbräu to get a midday meal. There we got some kind of sauce and coal-black dumplings.[107]

Nine days later, American troops entered the town, encountering no resistance.

After the war: US canteen and the "Schnöll era"

From the end of the war until 1955 the town of Salzburg was the headquarters of the American occupation zone, which comprised the Provinces of Salzburg and Upper Austria (except the Mühlviertel district). For this reason alone, the presence of the United States Forces in Austria (USFA) had a strong influence on the economic, cultural and social life of the town. Points of contact between the population and the representatives of the occupying power were on many levels – in both positive and negative aspects –, although the everyday life of the Americans and the local residents ultimately went on in two completely separate spheres.[1]

Immediately after the war had ended, many public buildings, inns and hotels and even private homes had been requisitioned for purposes of accommodation, work and leisure. The majority of the homes and many businesses were returned by the end of 1945, but inns and hotels remained under US administration, and were often returned only after several years – some not until 1955.[2] These included large hotels such as the *Österreichischer Hof*, and the *Stein* and *Bristol* hotels. Coffee-houses such as *Mozart* and *Tomaselli* were also used by the US army – the latter temporarily known as "Forty-Second Street Café".[3]

The Sternbräu, too, was requisitioned by the Americans and for the ensuing four years was compulsorily removed from the Salzburg gastronomic world. The restaurant

In 1995, the 1920s ballroom/dining-room became the *Stern Theatre*, and from 2000 the *Stern Saal*, scene of performances such as the „Sound of Music Show". It is now the *SternLounge*.

complex was eminently serviceable, although the building at Griesgasse 25 had been destroyed in a bomb attack. The ruin was to remain so for the ensuing years, but at least it was given protection – for which, in October 1945, the Stadtbauamt [municipal planning and building control office] allotted the company 423 m² sheet iron, 18 m³ construction timber, 30 kg nails, 400 kg building cement and 9,700 bricks, allowing the construction of several shed roofs to cover the ruins.[4]

The intact public rooms were used on the one hand for USFA activities, and on the other to provide the Austrian civilian employees of the occupying power with daily meals. There was great demand for Austrian employees, and the well-paid jobs with the Americans were much sought-after. Jobs with the "Amis" included chauffeurs, lorry-drivers, mechanics, warehousemen, canteen staff, receptionists, interpreters and office-workers.[5] One contemporary witness remembers: *The whole of the Sternbräu was requisitioned and was a huge canteen for Austrians working for the Americans.*[6] The Sternbräu was also used for frequent official functions, mostly concerning the occupying power in some way. Leave-taking ceremonies, for example. *A festive company assembled in the "Sternbräu" restaurant* on 14 December 1945, to bid farewell to the departing superintendent of the American military police, Colonel Edward Bolzendahl.[7] In May 1946 a farewell ball was organised in the Sternbräu for Captain Kannengiesser, head of the censor's office. According to one newspaper report, *Capt. Martin Kannengiesser was one of the most popular department heads.*[8] Besides the ball in the Sternbräu, his Austrian employees organised a bus trip to the

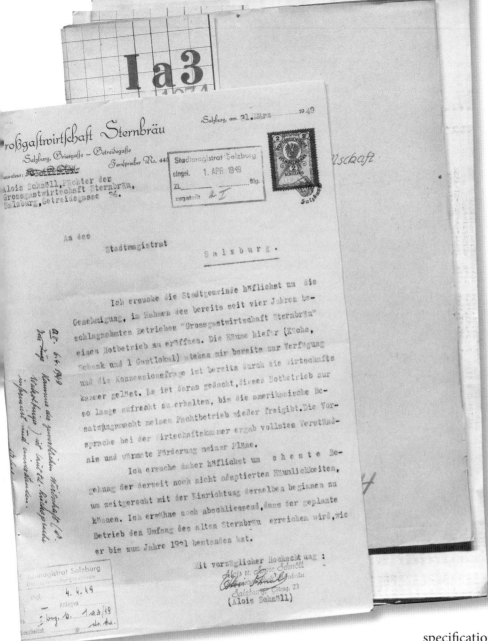

Request from lessee Alois Schnöll to the town council, for permission to run a "contingency operation" in the building at Getreidegasse 34, since the premises on the Griesgasse had been requisitioned by the American forces.

Salzkammergut and a private performance in the Landestheater. In November 1947, on the other hand, there was an exclusively Salzburg-related event: *It was a celebration of rebirth, when in recent days the municipal employees' wind band gave its inaugural concert.*[9] The location was *the jam-packed Sternbräu.*[10]

Alois Schnöll, the last lessee before the requisitioning, wanted to run his restaurant again. In March 1949 he applied for permission to run a so-called "contingency operation" in the original public rooms of the Sternbräu at Getreidegasse 34–36, which had been closed since 1932. On headed notepaper of the *Grossgastwirtschaft Sternbräu*, which still bore the name of his predecessor Karl Ohneiser as restaurateur, Schnöll conveyed his request to the town council. In these premises, which consisted of only kitchen, bar and one public room, he intended *to keep a contingency operation going until the American occupying power releases my leased premises again.*[11] Since the old public house had not existed as such for 17 years, it first had to be repaired and put back into operation according to the council's specifications. Among other things, the flooring of the public room had to be treated with dust-binder oil, *in order to rid the room of the dreadful accumulation of dust after it had stood empty for years.*[12] In the context of this contingency operation, which started at the beginning of

Salzburg inns and restaurants requisitioned and used by the USFA from 1945, with the date of their return:

30.11.1945: Café *Bazar*

15.12.1945: Café *Mozart* (used as officers' club for the Rainbow Division)

14.07.1947: Café *Lohr*

10.11.1948: Hotel *Traube*

01.10.1949: Grossgasthof *Sternbräu* (re-opening)

15.12.1949: *Gablerbräu* (re-opening)

28.07.1950: Café *Tomaselli* (re-opening)

01.05.1950: Hotel *Stein* (used as accommodation for the US military police)

15.12.1950: Hotel *Kasererhof* (re-opening; first returned at the beginning of 1948, re-requisitioned in May 1948 for the Russians, evacuated in June 1950 by the Soviet Repatriation Commission, old wing used by US military police until July 1953)

08.01.1951: Gasthof *Hofwirt* (re-opening)

10.11.1952: Hotel *Pitter* (partial return)

08.04.1955: *Gablerbräu-Bräusstübl* (restitution took place after the NCOs' club *The Rocker* moved to the former *Casanova* cabaret at Plainstrasse 3 (*Innsbrucker Hof*); re-opening 7.12.1955)

19.09.1955: Hotel *Bristol* (restitution)

24.09.1955: Hotel Österreichischer Hof (restitution)

24.09.1955: Hotel *Pitter* (restitution of the section of the hotel reserved for the USFA)

30.12.1955: Café *Glockenspiel* (re-opening)

June 1949, we learn something about the dimensions of this room – which is interesting, since we have neither views nor plans of this original Sternbräu tavern. The premises were on the first floor; the public room was 14.5m long and 5 m wide, so had a considerable floor area of 72.5m², and was 2.6m high. This was the dining-room, for the public bar was originally on the ground floor, on the right of the passage to the courtyard.

Temporary arrangements often develop an astonishing longevity – but not in this case. The interlude as an American canteen ended for the Sternbräu after a little more than four years, on 31 August 1949, so the public house in the Getreidegasse was ultimately in operation for only three months.

During the whole of September 1949 *work went on day and night*[13] – a total of 20 firms were involved in the restoration work to re-open the Sternbräu as soon as possible.

On Saturday 1 October 1949 the moment had come: large newspaper advertisements announced that the Sternbräu at Griesgasse 23 (telephone number 1440) was now open for business. The *cosy bars, the fine dining-room and* Bürgersaal, *this last decorated with the massive paintings by Karl Reisenbichler, are back again in all their glory.*[14] The public was also reminded that they were *welcome to consume food they had brought with them.*[15] Landlord Alois Schnöll directed a staff of 75, *for whom the best is only just good enough.*[16] For this practised restaurateur –

Single-column report in the *Salzburger Nachrichten*, 1 October 1949, on the re-opening of the Sternbräu.

Großgasthof „Sternbräu" eröffnet

Im Großgasthof „Sternbräu" in der Griesgasse wurde seit drei Wochen Tag und Nacht gearbeitet. Über zwanzig Firmen waren an den Wiederherstellungsarbeiten beteiligt. Nun ist das Werk vollendet. Die 1931 durch einen großzügigen Umbau geschaffenen gemütlichen Bierstuben, der schöne Speise- und Bürgersaal, letzterer geschmückt mit den wuchtigen Bildern von Karl Reisenbichler aus der ereignisschweren Stadtgeschichte, sowie alle anderen Räume sind wieder in alter Pracht erstanden. Heute konnte nach jahrelanger Unterbrechung der „Sternbräu" wieder seine gastlichen Pforten öffnen. Die Brauerei selbst, die einst auf dem Platze stand, auf dem sich heute der schattige Gastgarten befindet, wurde vermutlich 1415 von Hans Hauswirl, genannt der „hülzen Schuster", gegründet.

attested the daily *Demokratisches Volksblatt – knows from long experience that loyalty can be demanded from staff only if they are well-treated.*[17]

Immediately after its re-opening, the *Stern*, with its bars, dining-rooms and gardens, was a gastronomic Mecca both for local residents and for visitors from all over the world. In his Salzburg guide published in 1954, Josef Kaut writes: *Among the many pubs, the Sternbräu, with its garden amid the old houses between Getreidegasse and Griesgasse, enjoys a special reputation.*[18] Thanks to the number of club-rooms available, the Sternbräu soon became a meeting-place for societies, clubs and political parties, where meetings, conventions, lectures and rallies were held. It was the scene of the founding of the Salzburg Luftsportverband [air sports association] and the annual convention of the Salzburg Heimatvereine [societies for the preservation of regional customs and traditions]. Here

the Austrian student corps assembled for a traditional ceremony, the Salzburg regional teachers' association was reconstituted, and the disability sports club held its meetings. Conspicuous at the beginning of the 1950s were the increased activities of the VdU [Federation of Independents – predecessors of the Freedom Party] and various German nationalist circles, which at this time held their functions in the Sternbräu. These included, for instance, the inaugural assemblies of the *Salzburger Akademiker-*

verband and the VdU youth organisation *Unabhängige Jugend Österreichs*, a protest demonstration by the VdU against US High Commissioner Walter J. Donnelly, and a rally of the *Movement for Political Renewal* by the far-right People's Party politician Ernst Strachwitz. We also learn of a meeting of Habsburg loyalists that took place in October 1954, led by schoolteacher Engelbert Pilshofer. The meeting was reported in a highly polemic article in the Socialist daily *Demokratisches Volksblatt*, which called Pilshofer a *Monarcho-Partisan* and identified the participants as *dolled-up little counts and baronesses*.[19]

Most of the functions held in the Sternbräu, however, had nothing to do with politics. They were either for entertainment, as the many (masked) balls during the carnival period, or informative (liqueur producer Oeller from Vienna offered a course on the right way to mix cocktails with milk).[20]

Sensations were on offer, too: *As from this afternoon, the fakir Rayo, famous in half Europe as "the man in the bottle", will be on display in his glass coffin, in the Sternbräu restaurant. On 13 December 1952, Rayo had himself enclosed in the 2.30m-high bottle of thick showcase glass – with the intention of not leaving it for three times 90 days … In his transparent coffin he subsists on only three vitamin pills a day and a little fruit. Since December, some 80,000 people in various European towns have marvelled at him.*[21] "Rayo" was in reality the Upper Austrian conjuror and entertainer Rudolf Schmid (1901–1979), who thrilled audiences with his unusual performances.[22]

On 16 March 1953 the *Salzburger Nachrichten* reported on the display by the fakir Rayo in the Sternbräu.

Der „Mann in der Flasche" in Salzburg

Der Fakir Rayo, in halb Europa als der „Mann in der Flasche" bekannt geworden, wird ab heute nachmittag im Großgasthof „Sternbräu" in seinem gläsernen Sarg zu sehen sein. Am 13. Dezember 1952 ließ sich Rayo in die 2.30 m hohe Flasche aus dickem Auslageglas einschließen — mit dem Willen, sie dreimal 90 Tage nicht zu verlassen. Nach jedem Turnus folgen einige Tage, in denen er leichte Schonkost zu sich nimmt. In seinem durchsichtigen Sarg ernährt er sich nur durch täglich drei Vitamintabletten und etwas Obst. Seit Dezember haben ihn etwa 80.000 Menschen in den verschiedensten europäischen Städten bestaunt.

The end of the Sternbrauerei

While the restaurant complex had been positively revitalised, on the other side of the Mönchsberg things were winding down. After only 49 years of operation, the Sternbrauerei in the Riedenburg was closed down at the end of 1956, bringing in-house beer production to an end after more than 400 years. Rationalisation measures implemented by the Österreichische Brau AG were given as the reason. The brewery had produced some 30,000 hectolitres of "Stern beer" annually. Arguments for the closure were the outdated plant, the high cost of modernisation and the fact that the far larger and more modern brewery in Kaltenhausen was only 15 kilometres away. Despite a promise that *even with production in Kaltenhausen … "Stern beer" would still be made*,[23] this was probably done only briefly. After a few years, the Sternbräu, too, served only beer from the Hofbräu Kaltenhausen. It is only since 2008 – and of course since the re-opening in autumn 2014 – that a specially-brewed "Stern beer" has been on offer again. Part of the decommissioned Riedenburg brewery was used as a depot, various premises were sold or rented out, and superfluous buildings demolished. In 1972 the 56m-high chimney was blasted, and for years this land in the shade of the Rainberg was practically a brownfield site, used by resourceful Salzburgers as an unofficial car park. A relict of the brewery days was the *Sternkeller* (opened in 1897) on the ground floor of the old brewhouse, now known as the *Altes Stern(gasthaus)*, or simply "Rosi", after the last landlady. This pub was popular for its cosy, old-fashioned rustical

Großgastwirtschaft Sternbräu Salzburg

GRIESGASSE GETREIDEGASSE FERNRUF 81440

A. u. A. SCHNÖLL

GANZTÄGIG WARME KÜCHE • EIGENE SCHLÄCHTEREI UND WURSTEREI

31. August 1958

SPEISE-KARTE

SUPPEN

Geb. Leberknödelsuppe	2.--
Fleischstrudelsuppe	1.50
Grießnockerl- oder Geflügelsuppe	1.50
Ungarische Gulyassuppe	2.--
Bouillon mit Ei	3.--
Würstelsuppe mit Nudeln	7.--

WARME VORSPEISEN

Champignon gebacken, Sce. tartare	12.--
Omelette mit Käse	10.--
Karfiol mit Butterbrösel	7.50
Ravioli	8.--
Schinkenspaghetti	7.50
Spinat mit Spiegelei	7.50

FISCHE

Forelle blau, zerlassene Butter, Kartoffel, per deka	1.20
Karpfen gebacken, Mayonnaisesalat	15.--
Karpfen blau, zerlassene Butter, Kartoffel,	16.--

FERTIGE SPEISEN

1/4 Ente, Knödel, Weinkraut	28.--
1/2 Brathuhn, Reis, gem. Salat	28.--
Port. Suppenhuhn mit Nudeln	12.--
Geflügelrisotto, Reibkäse, Salat	12.--
Bauernschmaus	18.--
Engl. Roastbeef, Erbsen, pom. frites	18.--
Gesp. Rehschlögl, Knödel, Preiselb.,	10.--
Rehragout mit Knödel	14.--
Eisbein, Sauerkraut, Salzkartoffel	13.--
Surbraten, Knödel, Rettichsalat	14.--
Hausgeselchtes, Sauerkraut, Knödel	13.--
Schweinskarree, Knödel, Specksalat	9.--
Szegedinergulyas mit Knödel	7.--
Schweinsbratwürstl, Sauerkr., Röstk.	7.--
Ung. Schweinskotelette, Nockerl, Sal.	17.--
Gefüllte grüne Paprika, Kartoffel	10.--
Ochsenfleisch, Spinat, Röstkartoffel	10.--
Gefüllte Kalbsbrust, Reis, Salat	10.--
Ochsenschlepp mit Knödel	8.--
Port. Kalbstelze fein garniert	15.--
Nierenbraten, Reis, gem. Salat	14.--
Champignonschnitzel, Reis, Salat	20.--
Zigeunerbraten, Reis, Salat	14.--
Kalbsgulyas mit Nockerl	11.--
Reisfleisch, Reibkäse, Salat	8.--
Paprikazüngerl mit Spaghetti	8.--
Kalbsbeuschel mit Knödel	6.--
Rahmrostbraten, Knödel, Gurkerl	15.--
Fasch. Butterschnitzel, Reis, Salat	8.--
Hausgemachte Krainer, Sauerkraut	6.--

SPEISEN AUF BESTELLUNG

1/2 Backhuhn, Kartoffel, gem. Salat	28.--
Sternspezialplatte	25.--
Schnitzel à la Holstein	22.--
Wienerschnitzel, Kartoffel, Salat	16.--
Pariserschnitzel, Reis, Kompott	20.--
Zwiebelrostbraten, Knödel, Gurkerl	15.--
Geröstete Leber, Kartoffelsalat	13.--
Kalbskopf gebacken, Kartoffelsalat	7.50
Schweinskotelette geb., Kart., Salat	16.--
Tirolergröstel, gemischt. Salat	6.50
Vom Grill: Mixed Grill	25.--
Serbischer Spieß auf Reis, Salat	17.--
Engl. Beefsteak, Ei, pommes frites	25.--

KALTE SPEISEN

Schwedenplatte	25.--
Hors d'oeuvres varies Toast	25.--
Kaltes Huhn garniert	28.--
Beefsteak tartare mit Ei	20.--
Kaltes Roastbeef, Sce. tartare	18.--
Sternplatte 15.-- Ung. Salami	15.--
Port. Presschinken mit Aspik	15.--
Kalter Schweinsbraten, Gurkerl	10.--
Rindfleisch in Essig und Öl	8.--
Pikante Kleinigkeiten	8.--
Russisches Ei garniert	7.--
Häuptelsalat mit Ei	6.--
Wurstplatte 7.-- Appetitbrot	5.50
It. Fleischsalat 6.50 Haussulze	4.--
Essigwurst 5.-- Ochsenmaulsalat	6.--
Thunfisch 8.-- Lachs auf Toast	6.--
Fischmayonnaise 10.-- Sardinen	5.--
Sardellenringerl mit Butter	4.--
Brathering oder Rollmops	3.--
Radies'chen mit Butter	

GEMÜSE UND BEILAGEN

Zuckererbsen	4.50	Peperoni-	3.--
Pommes frites	3.--	Weisskraut	3.--
Sce. tartare	3.--	Karotten-	3.--
Semmelknödel	1.50	Reis-	3.--
Heurige Kartoffel-			2.--

SALATE

		Salatplatte	6.--
		Grüner Bohnen-	5.--
Französischer-	4.--	Tomaten-	4.--
Mayonnaise-	4.--	Karfiol-	4.--
Gemischter-	3.--	Gurken-	3.--
Kartoffel-	3.--	Häuptel-	3.--
Kraut-	3.--		

KOMPOTTE

Gemischtes Kompott	5.--
Ringlottenkompott	5.--
Aprikosen- oder Kirschenkompott	5.--
Birnen- oder Apfelkompott	5.--
Preiselbeerkompott	5.--

MEHLSPEISEN

Salzburg. Nockerl	16.--
Malakowtorte	6.20
Erdbeertorte mit Schlag	6.20
Sacher od. Haselnusstorte, Schlag	5.70
Schokolade- od. Cafecremetorte	5.70
Nusskipferl od. Makronenschnitte	5.--
Biscuitrolle od. Indianer m. Schlag	4.50
Apfelstrudel mit Schlag	4.50
Punschkrapferl /Schokoladedessert	3.50
Ischlerkrapferl	2.50
Rehrücken od. Baiser mit Schlag	4.50
Ananasscheiben mit Schlag	7.50
Palatschinken mit Aprikosen	7.50
Kaiserschmarren mit Rosinen	9.50
Omelette Confiture	16.--
Omelette à la Stefanie	
Eis: Kaffee, Orange, Vanille	
Früchte-Eisbecher 8.50 Eiskaffee	7.--
Gem. Eis m. Schlag 5.-- 1 Eistüte	--.50
Omelette Surprise f. 2 Personen	22.--

KAFFEE

1 kleiner Espresso	2.50
1 grosser Espresso	5.--
1 Kaffee mit Milch	3.50

KÄSE

Käseplatte mit Butter	10.--
Gorgonzola m. Butter passiert	6.--
Emmenthaler- oder Mondseer-	4.--
Achleitner/Schloss/Camenbert-	3.50
Portion Quargeln mit Butter	1.80
Liptauer- 3.-- Port. Butter	2.50

Zuzüglich 10% Bedienung

---

ambience, with a garden shaded by chestnut trees and an open pavilion. In 2007 the "Rosi" finally had to close its doors. Since 2005, the site had already had a new owner, to be followed at short intervals by others. 2007 saw the construction of an exclusive residential complex (with corresponding purchase prices), the former brewery wing being retained and renovated.

Ox meat and fish mayonnaise

Over the course of the 1950s, in keeping with the population's growing desire for consumption, the tables of catering establishments once more groaned under the weight of "status food" no. 1: meat. Menus read as though the years of privation were to be compensated within the shortest possible period. Depending on staff and kitchen potential, Salzburg restaurants once more served ample meals with meat predominant on the menu.

Quantity was the main thing; quality was closely linked to the quantity of what was on the menu. The Sternbräu kitchen also offered an incredible variety of dishes, compared with today. The menu of 31 August 1958, for instance, had 6 kinds of soup, 6 hot starters, 3 fish dishes, 29 ready-to-serve dishes, 13 dishes to order, 20 cold dishes, 9 vegetable and other side-dishes, 11 salads, 7 compotes and 22 desserts. Of the 42 ready-to-serve dishes and dishes to order, not a single one was meatless. There was *marinated pot-roast, Szegedin goulash, rack of pork, ox-tail, kidney roast, tongue with paprika,*

Menu, 31 August 1958: 42 main dishes – and not a single meatless one.

baked *calf's-head* and *larded leg of venison*. The menus in comparable restaurants looked similar. The Sternbräu had its own slaughterhouse and charcuterie production, where whole animals were processed, partly because pre-portioned meat was not yet customary, and partly because offal, for instance, was in keeping with current taste.

We have Harald Engländer (at that time landlord of the *Höllbräu*) to thank for some interesting marginalia on the kitchen and general course of business in the Sternbräu. Engländer visited numerous competitors to see what their menus offered, and made notes after these "espionage excursions". He paid a visit to the Sternbräu on 2 November 1958: *The Stern is very busy. Lots of country folk, and even if the sale of frankfurters was booming, schnitzel, various roasts and other freshly-cooked dishes were still popular orders. Regrettably, in such a large establishment the lack of training is all too evident in the majority of the new staff.*[24] Three days later, he found the restaurant *well attended*, and on 10 November the visitor numbers in all the places he visited were *very good*. Engländer was particularly interested in the set meals, which differed substantially in price from the à-la-carte menus. On 5 November 1958, the Sternbräu offered two set meals, one at 8 schillings (Backerbsensuppe [broth with fried soup pearls], home-made leberwurst with sauté potatoes and sauerkraut) and one at 11 schillings (mushroom soup, roast veal, macaroni, *Polsterzipf* [a sweet pastry] with raspberry juice). Engländer noted that the latter menu was more popular: *The 11-schilling was especially popular, the meat was a good helping and macaroni as side-dish was ample. The* Polsterzipfe *looked very good – a popular dessert worth copying.*[25] He found no words of praise, however, for the "fried brains with egg" offered on the menu: *... rather too small a helping for 13.–, a little round bowl with the egg-yolk in the middle. In my own experience, this way of serving it is not as popular and filling as when the brains are mixed with the egg and fried more like an omelette.*[26] Voilà!

Reconstruction and change of landlord

While the catering business had been flourishing for a decade, the ravages of the bombing were still to be seen in the building at Griesgasse 25. The irreparable parts of the ruin had been cleared in 1950, but an unsightly gap remained.

In November 1959 Salzburg's mayor, Alfred Bäck, wrote to the Österreichische Brau AG with the urgent request *to find some urbanistically satisfactory solution for the disgraceful state of things that still exists in the Griesgasse, almost 15 years after the end of the war, and to undertake the rectification of this matter as soon as possible.*[27] The Brau AG, however, showed no particular interest in the "rectification of this matter", stating in justification that *it has stretched resources to the utmost, simply to get the business up and running again.*[28] Moreover, they said bluntly in their reply, *there is no operational necessity for rebuilding the object with several storeys.*[29] The town thereupon sent the Brau AG an official notification to the effect that the parts of the building that were in danger of collapse must

The bombed-out shell of Griesgasse 23 (photo taken in January 1956).

Griesgasse 25, completed in 1963, is a typical
example of the architecture of the day.

View of the bombed-out shell and the gap,
as seen from the high school (now AVA Hof).

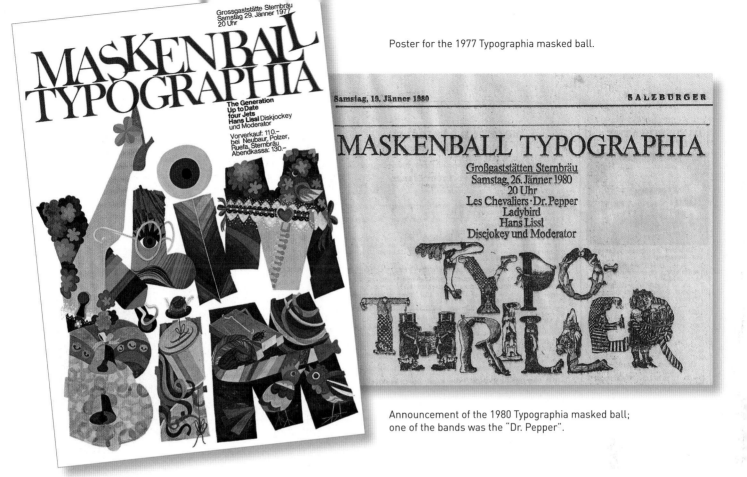

Poster for the 1977 Typographia masked ball.

Announcement of the 1980 Typographia masked ball;
one of the bands was the "Dr. Pepper".

be secured or removed, and that *within 3 months from the service of this writ, a proposal for the definitive restoration or reconstruction of the bombed building must be submitted to the building inspectorate of Salzburg town council.*[30] This at last brought results, and in 1962 reconstruction was begun. By December 1963, a new building of the same height adjoined the remaining one at Griesgasse 23. The Sterngässchen entrance was overbuilt and a passageway added.

In the ground floor of the new building, the Brau AG installed an additional public room, the *particularly tastefully furnished "Kaltenhausener Bierstuben"*. In a press re-

lease, they declared themselves delighted to have *afforded the town of Salzburg an agreeable Christmas surprise.*[31] On the first floor of the building were extra club-rooms for private functions. The *Kaltenhausener Bierstuben* was replaced in 1979 by Salzburg's first beer-pub, called the *Braumeister*.

On 1 October 1959 Johann and Hilde Stadler took over the Sternbräu, and ran the restaurant for 19 successful years. In contrast to previous decades, the 1960s and '70s were marked by an unprecedented continuity. The Sternbräu had survived all the major rebuilding, conversion and renovation, and the Stadlers could concentrate on the

Typical crush shortly before the opening of the Lions Club flea market in the restaurant garden, 1990s.

business in hand. *Now Hans Stadler, a trained chef and one of the best landlords in Salzburg, is the lessee. This is why the restaurant is flourishing, this is why one does not have the feeling of being a mere number, in this extensive establishment with perhaps a thousand patrons over midday.*[32] During these years, then, the restaurant was always a gastronomic Mecca in the Old Town, while remaining a popular venue for all kinds of events, ranging from the legendary masked balls held by the Typographia male-voice choir

(the so-called "Typo-Gschnase", at which one of the present authors used to perform with his international dance and show band "Dr. Pepper") to the annual flea market organised by the Hohensalzburg Lions Club.

Starting in 1963, the annual Lions flea market was held fifty times in the Sternbräu, until 2012, the year before the most recent reconstruction.

Continuity is also apparent on the culinary side. A comparison of the menus from 1958 and 1967 shows that the range on offer was slightly less, but the choice of dishes was practically unchanged. Of the six "hot starters", four were identical (apart from the prices), and for the "ready-to-serve dishes" 18 were the same on the two menus.

While the price for ¼ duck with dumplings and salad, and for ½ roast chicken with rice and salad remained the same at 28 schillings, the Wiener schnitzel had increased from 16 to 26 schillings, the Szegedin goulash from 9 to 15 schillings, and the stuffed breast of veal from 10 to 19 schillings. New items on the menu included a genuine turtle soup (in cup) at 12 schillings, curried boneless veal-leg roast with rice and salad at 25 schillings and baked calf's-feet with mayonnaise salad at 12 schillings.

Towards the end of the 1960s, the large self-service restaurant garden became a popular meeting-place for a developing youth culture. Hair was worn longer, the atmosphere was more colourful. *It's a lively scene in the summer months, with many different languages and nationalities mingling beneath the old trees. Then at times the merry sing-song may even drown out the noise of the traffic.*[33] Besides the central location, the reasonable prices account for this: *There's draught beer in self-service, and people can eat food they've brought with them at the large tables. ... So young people who are hard up like to gather at the Sternbräu.*[34]

Menu, 4 November 1967.

129

Memories of the Sternbräu: 1971/72

It's impossible to say exactly when we daring students first visited the Sternbräu garden to pour beer into our young, unhabituated bodies. We were certainly not yet 16 – it was probably 1971 – and we were in the 5b class at the Akademisches Gymnasium. The location of the Sternbräu was strategically convenient for us. At that time the school was still in the old building on the Universitätsplatz, and we had only to hurry through a passageway, cross the Getreidegasse and there we were, right in the centre of the gastronomic life of the Old Town. Afternoon classes were to blame for the whole thing, because we were condemned to explore the environs of the school during the lunch break, with eyes open and minds alert. Within a radius of 300 metres we investigated every shop with earnest thoroughness – from Stumpp seed-shop to Slama clothing-store, from Bally shoe-shop to Roittner ironmongers. Our midday meal consisted of either gobbling down a spicy hot-dog from the buffet of the non-stop cinema or (a great alternative!) enjoying 100g fish with potato salad at "Fisch-Krieg". Sometimes during the warmer days we landed, clutching our delicacies, in the Sternbräu garden

End of term, 1972: l. to r.: Blacky, Nudl, Porridge, Laschuor, Oster and Steini.

– the self-service one (we never went inside). My first half-litre, which I fetched from the bar and paid for myself, cost 3.90 schillings, though the price soon jumped to 4.50 schillings. At first, we got quite merry after just half a litre, and we hadn't really developed a taste for beer yet, so we never had more than one. Even then, I used to wonder what our music teacher must have thought when the atmosphere in the music-room started took on the aroma of fish, sausage and beer after we came in.

Since the end of the 1960s, the Sternbräu garden had developed into a popular meeting-place for young people.

The Sternbräu garden was filled with a motley crowd, much to the chagrin of Herr Stadler. As lessee and landlord, he often had to intervene personally in order to calm things down at one table or other. It was here that I first saw the consequences of demon drink: before the astonished eyes of an adolescent youth, two brawlers went for each other, soon grabbing glass beer-mugs to hit each other over the head. Once again, Herr Stadler intervened and separated the two, who then looked pretty stupid as they were subjected to a good dressing-down ("Next time, you're banned!", or something similar), until they were reduced to maudlin tears, and ended up locked in an emotional embrace. When I told my father this amazing story the same evening, he was unimpressed and simply muttered: "Drunks!"

At the end of the school year, after the reports had been given out, the summer holidays traditionally started in the Sterngarten. To mark this fine day, we might drink two or even three half-litres, as long as we weren't overtaken by incipient nausea. After this "symposium", it was clear that one or other school report was no longer entirely legible, and one in fact went missing altogether.

A lively mixture of students from various schools was to be found here. Since the Sternbräu was trapped, so to speak, between the Akademisches Gymnasium on the Universitätsplatz and the high school on the Hanuschplatz, we soon got to know one another, and – as I forgot to mention, but the gentle reader will surely realise – the Sternbräu collective of the 15- and 16-year-olds was exclusively male territory. Before winter came, the Sterngarten was put out of commission and all packed up; the round table-tops were removed, leaving only the concrete stands, the tops of which were flat crosses with slits in them. One Stern buddy, Didi S., dubbed this unintentional, uniform sculpture park a "drunks' cemetery". This epithet was probably the reason for the entire garden being remodelled in 1986/87. After its re-opening, the 5b Sterngarten days were well and truly past.

From the collected writings of H. W.
(manuscript in the possession of the authors)

Autumn melancholy in the Sternbräu garden, November 1979.

Project: "Vitalising the Sternbräu"

On 1 November 1978, Günter Puttinger became the new Sternbräu landlord. Son-in-law of his predecessor Johann Stadler, he already knew the restaurant, and he continued to run it for 28 years after he took it over.

During this period the Sternbräu underwent a whole series of innovations which had a lasting effect on the business. From the start, Puttinger focused on "the gastronomic experience". He considered the Sternbräu simply too large for the gastronomic concept of a large restaurant offering good plain cooking. His aim was to combine different styles of cuisine under one roof. The first step (as mentioned above) was to convert the *Kaltenhausener Bierstuben* into Salzburg's first beer pub, called the *Braumeister*.

This was in keeping with the current trend. Alongside the hearty beer-drinking tradition, a lighter, more lively atmosphere took hold in the gastronomic world.

The longest interruption in Puttinger's time at the Sternbräu was for the alterations carried out in 1986/87. On 27 February 1986, the Österreichische Brau AG presented the project "Vitalising the Sternbräu". A project description designed for the media started by describing the initial situation, which – as was the intention – did not look at all good. The guest should not have to put up with the view into the large outdoor area during the winter months: *He has to stare at those offputting cumbersome walls surrounding the garden, the windowless façade of the old malt-house and the featureless front of the kitchen wing* – an unacceptable view.[35] It could *not, therefore, be imagined that our guest, confronted with this view, can feel any kind of aesthetic inspiration.*[36] The planners were chiefly concerned to enliven the large garden all year round, and to achieve *an improved architectural impression of the entire area in the process.*[37] The *Salzburger Nachrichten* reported: *Through*

Günter Puttinger, Sternbräu landlord 1978–2005.

Salzburg's first beer pub, called *Braumeister*, opened in 1979; shown here in the 1990s.

Model for the planned alterations in 1986/87. These include a pavilion in the large garden and an additional storey on the wing between Getreidegasse and Griesgasse.

the old Tränktor to the beer garden[38], the *Salzburger Tagblatt* had the heading *Aesthetics for brewery guests*,[39] and the title page of the *Neue Salzburg Krone* announced: *Stern garden becomes a shopping passage.*[40] The *Krone* resident poet Theo Renzl penned the following:

Der Sternbräugartn is koa Schund,	*The Sternbräu garden isn't trashy,*
den machn s' jetzt ganz neu und rund!	*they're making it all new and flashy!*
Und d' Leut, de rennan, wia ma woaß,	*And folks'll hustle, fit to burst,*
wanns sein muaß, ah um's Bier im	*to get their beer when they've a thirst!*
Kroas![41]	

Construction work began on 13 October 1986, after the traditional flea market of the Hohensalzburg Lions Club, held that year on 27 May, and continued until spring 1987. The most noticeable changes around the large garden were the removal of the bar and the surrounding wall built in 1950, the conversion of the arcades and the pavilion into shops, and a pavilion for serving food and drinks in the middle of the garden. The wing facing the restaurant garden had an upper storey and old-style arcades added, and an open bandstand was built in the restaurant garden itself. The rather unattractive "Laubenraum" [summerhouse], whose walls were decorated in 1931 by the painter Theodor Kern, was converted into a separately-run trattoria significantly called *La Stella* (which was then moved into the former malt-house as part of the 2013/2014 conversion).

In order to establish a link with the 15th-century town wall, a second gateway was built at the site of the old wall, after the Griesgasse entrance, designed to represent the ancient "lower *Tränktor*" – to the delight of Johannes Voggenhuber, the town councillor responsible.[42]

Through his involvement in business and politics, Puttinger achieved for the Sternbräu a reputation that went far beyond Salzburg. First, he chaired the tourism department of the Salzburg Chamber of Commerce (1988–1990),

The trattoria *La Stella* opened in 1987, in place of a summerhouse. In the course of the major reconstruction in 2013/14 it was moved into the former malt-house.

The "lower *Tränktor*" (in the background), built in 1986/87 to represent the 15th-century location of the town wall. Here was a gateway (*Tränktor*) through to the Salzach and to a watering-place for cattle.

Sincere Remorse

In October 1982, the Sternbräu received an unusual letter. The sender, who signed himself F.A.O., confessed that in 1948 – 34 years previously – he had "forgotten" to pay his bill at the Sternbräu, and now wished to do penance and make good the debt. 500 schillings were enclosed in the letter, which read:

To the
Sternbräu

5020 Salzburg
Sterngässchen

Vienna, 7 October 1982

To the management:

As a young man of around 19 in 1948, I ate and drank my fill at the Sternbräu – I had Bauernschmaus [farmer's platter] and drinks – without paying.

Today I would like to apologise for this behaviour, and I enclose S 500.-- as compensation for the wrongdoing of a stupid, harebrained youth.

Please accept this belated compensation as my sincere remorse.

I remain
Yours anonymously
F.A.O.
Enclosed: S 500.--

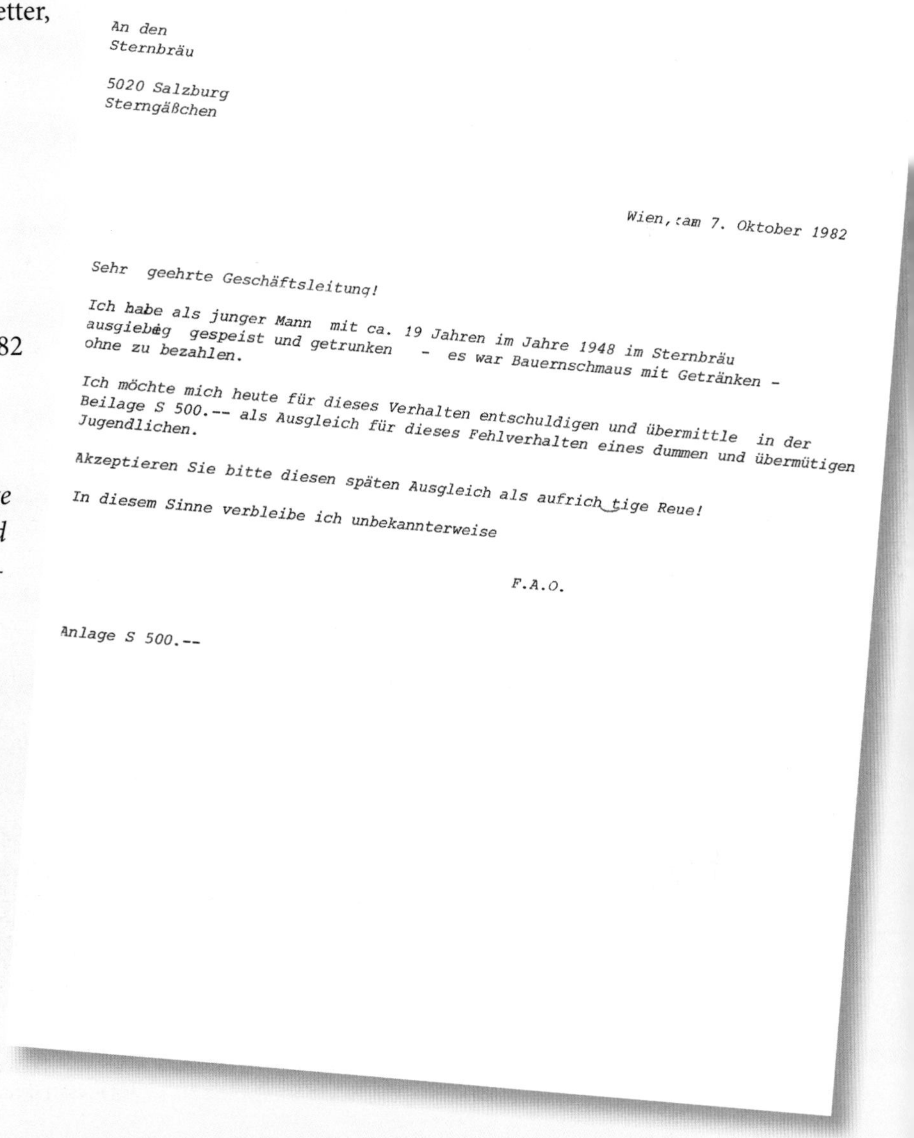

An den
Sternbräu

5020 Salzburg
Sterngäßchen

Wien, am 7. Oktober 1982

Sehr   geehrte Geschäftsleitung!

Ich habe als junger Mann mit ca. 19 Jahren im Jahre 1948 im Sternbräu ausgiebig gespeist und getrunken   - es war Bauernschmaus mit Getränken - ohne zu bezahlen.

Ich möchte mich heute für dieses Verhalten entschuldigen und übermittle in der Beilage S 500.-- als Ausgleich für dieses Fehlverhalten eines dummen und übermütigen Jugendlichen.

Akzeptieren Sie bitte diesen späten Ausgleich als aufrichtige Reue!

In diesem Sinne verbleibe ich unbekannterweise

F.A.O.

Anlage S 500.--

Günter Puttinger, Sternbräu landlord 1978-2006, checking orders received.

President of the ÖVP-Wirtschaftsbund [economic branch of the Austrian People's Party], losing the vote in 1999 to Christoph Leitl. His political involvement took him as ÖVP representative into the National Assembly (1993–2001). Asked how he managed to combine all these functions, he once replied: *"It's all a question of organisation. I've never had a problem about delegating. You have to be able to rely on people – and to trust them. Then it all works splendidly."*[43] As landlord and President of the Chamber of Commerce, he occasionally found himself in confrontation with the union – as on 12 March 1998, when at 11 a.m. 400 trade unionists from all over Austria occupied the Sternbräu and remained sitting at the tables for two hours over a so-called "minimum consumption". *Each one of you orders only one drink – then the landlords can see what it's like to earn so little*, said Rudolf Kaske, then chair of the Union of Hotel, Restaurant and Personal Service Workers.[44] This demonstration was intended to raise awareness of the poor working conditions and minimum wages (no increase in two years) in the hospitality sector.

then that of the Federal Chamber of Commerce (1990–1994), becoming President of the Salzburg Chamber of Commerce in 1994 (until 2000). In addition, during the period 1991-1999 he was President of the Austrian Association for Applied Tourism, deputy chair of the Austrian National Tourist Office, deputy chair of the board of the Salzburg Exhibition Centre and chair of the Society of Salzburg Schools of Tourism, though he never became

In Puttinger's day, besides normal business there were not only the traditional balls and *Gschnase*, but also many information events and discussion series on local and

The two gardens in the 1990s. The catering pavilion and the bandstand have both disappeared.

From 2000 onwards part of the standard repertoire in the *Sternsaal*: the Sound of Music Show.

Pre-Christmas activity: the Advent market in the *Sterngarten*.

socio-political topics. Socialist Youth, Salzburg Women's Cultural Centre, local government representatives and non-party platforms held lectures and debates in the Sternbräu, with one particular topic conspicuous during the 1990s: traffic. The discussions on mobility in the town of Salzburg focused on aspects including cycle paths, bus lanes and traffic-calming, tramway projects, shuttle-buses and speed limits. A further series of events consisted of theatrical performances. In 1995, the Sternbräu became the adopted home of Agilo and Christa Dangl's theatre group "Karawane", which twice a year gave a run of performances in the dining-room, temporarily transformed into the "Stern Theatre".

Starting in 2000, the newly-adapted room re-named the *Sternsaal* opened for the tourist "Sound of Music Show" and other theatre and cabaret performances. And from 1997, the Sternbräu grounds offered a further, pre-Christmas attraction, with the charming Advent arts & crafts market in the garden.

On 9 November 1998, for exceptional services to the Austrian economy the Sternbräu was awarded the right to bear the Austrian national coat of arms. On the same day, Günter Puttinger received the honorary title of *Kommerzialrat* [= councillor of commerce].

A new generation: at the beginning of 2006, Harald Kratzer took over the Sternbräu from Günter Puttinger.

Left: Beer garden summer party, 2007; here the band "Dino & die Saurier", which included the present author Gerhard Ammerer and *Stern* landlord Harald Kratzer.
Top left: Poster for the beer garden summer party in June 2007.
Top right: Poster (2009)advertising live music events in the Sternbräu.

Changes in ownership, change of lessee and new circumstances

In the first decade of the 21st century, the Sternbräu changed hands twice. This was due to the development of the Österreichische Brau AG, which had since 1929 owned the Sternbräu property. Their takeover of the Steirerbrau (Gösser, Reininghaus, Puntigamer) resulted in 1993 in the formation of the Brau Union AG, and in 1998 the Brau Union Österreich AG, which in turn merged in 2003 with the Dutch Heineken concern. In the course of these changes, the Brau Union parted with its non-essential real estate. A total of 78 properties – including the Sternbräu – were taken over by the real estate investment company CA Immo,[45] which did not intend to keep these properties. Only four years later, in spring 2009, no less than three old-established Salzburg brewery restaurants belonging to the former Brau AG changed hands at one stroke: the Sternbräu in the Griesgasse, the *Gablerbräu* in the Linzer Gasse and the *Zipfer Bierhaus* on the Universitätsplatz were sold to the property developer Immobilien Bauträger AG (IBT), owned by the Modrian and Neumayr families.

In this turbulent period, the Sternbräu had also a new lessee. In 2006, Günter Puttinger was succeeded as landlord by Harald Kratzer, who had already worked for a long time for Puttinger and the Sternbräu, but who did not originally come from the hospitality sector. Kratzer (*b* 1963) had studied journalism and political science, and had worked in marketing and the media. Through Günter Puttinger, who was looking for a marketing professional, Kratzer came to the Sternbräu in 1999, became an authorised signatory and finally manager. Although his training lay outside the industry, he still *cannot imagine a more exciting job, for this business never gets boring.*[46] His declared aim was to expand the target groups and to attract more young people. So by means of summer parties, music events, a Sternbräu regular customers card and the reintro-

The "Sternbräu-Gastronomiewelt" on signboards, in the pre-2012 design.

duction of a "Stern beer" specially brewed in Kaltenhausen, Kratzer brought new momentum to the Sternbräu, while retaining its traditional ambience.

In keeping with Günter Puttinger's idea of combining several styles of cuisine under one roof, in 2007 Harald Kratzer opened the trendy *Abendstern* bar, with subdued music and a good selection of wines. In 2011 a further room was added, which he called *Gwölb an der Stadtmauer* [vault by the town wall].

Soon it was clear that the IBT, together with Kratzer, had in mind a further development of the Sternbräu property, which would not be possible without reconstruction. The longer they went on "developing", the more comprehensive

Harald Kratzer, manager of the old and the new Sternbräu.

the reconstruction plans became. By the time the officially approved version of the mega-project (relative to the scale of the Old Town) was on the table, time had flown past, and it was 2012.

The Sternbräu was faced with the most extensive alterations for 82 years. On Saturday 5 January 2013, one more big party was held. *On Saturday, at a farewell party for the Sternbräu as we know it, some 150 guests celebrated, albeit* *with mixed feelings,*[47] we read, under the optimistic headline *Cheerful Farewell for 18 Months.*[48] In the end, the 18 months stretched to 21 – but then the Sternbräu rose again from the dust and rubble, and proudly presented itself to a marvelling public. On 23 October 2014 the long-awaited opening celebration was held, under the apt motto:

Der Stern geht wieder auf! The star rises again!

Amazement, doubts, good wishes
Major reconstruction – modest beginnings

1 Summary of the report by archaeologists Ulli Hampel and Birgit Niedermayr, Firma Ardig. Archäologischer Dienst GesmbH (with thanks for lending the manuscript), article by Peter Höglinger, *Die Stadtmauer im Sternbräu*, and newspaper article: *Alte Stadtmauer freigelegt*, in: Salzburger Nachrichten. *Aus Stadt und Land*, 7 March 2013, pp 1 & 12 f.

2 Cf. Ammerer/Baumgartner, *Die Getreidegasse*, p 202.

3 Quoted after AStS, building documentation, Getreidegasse 34, Sternbräu.

4 Cf. Dopsch/Hoffmann, *Geschichte der Stadt Salzburg*, p 155.

5 Cf. ebd., p 164.

6 Cf. ebd., p 281

7 Cf. in detail: Kohl, *Stockwerkseigentum*.

8 Quoted after AStS, building documentation, Getreidegasse 34, Sternbräu.

9 *Wolfganng Schwingenhaimer zu Trätmansperg* is also mentioned as surety in a letter of patronage dated 12 September 1546 (cf. SLA, OU 1546 IX 12).

10 AStS, Bruderhaus account book 756, 1542: *Vermerckht ain Ausgab vnd zue des paungartners spenndt khauf wie hernach.*

11 Cf. Zillner, *Geschichte I*, p 376.

12 Quoted after SLA, Doppler-Chronik 351. a.

13 Cf. Zillner, *Geschichte I*, p 376, note 1.

14 Cf. Kramml, *Bruderhaus*, pp 126 & 129.

15 Ammerer/Waitzbauer, *Wege zum Bier*, pp 12 & 16.

16 Cf. SLA, Doppler-Chronik 351. a.

17 SLA, Doppler-Chronik 351.

18 Privy archives of the Province of Salzburg, visitation of the town, 1569: on the first floor overlooking the Salzach live Georg Praunseisen, his wife, his son and a servant, on the second floor the messenger Heinrich Mayburger with wife and son, next door Ehrentraud Stauffner occupies one room, a further room is occupied by Anna Schurrin, an elderly seamstress, overlooking the Getreidegasse lives the aged widower Lamprecht Lindner, a former watchman on Hohensalzburg.

19 SLA, Doppler-Chronik 351.

20 SLA, Doppler-Chronik 351.

21 Cf. SLA, Doppler-Chronik 351. 6. The year of purchase, 1570, is evidently erroneoùs (v. Bürgerspital accounts).

22 SLA, Doppler-Chronik 351.

23 The tax register for 1608, however, shows one Jacob Erlacher as landlord; SLA, Doppler-Chronik 351. a.

24 Cf. Hauthaler/Martin, *Salzburger Urkundenbuch*, vol. I: *Traditionscodices*, Salzburg 1910, no. 471b, p 507 f.

25 Zillner, *Geschichte der Stadt Salzburg II.*, p 148.

26 Trade was making Salzburg wealthy, which encouraged the citizens to strive for more political independence. However, the rights of a free imperial town, conferred on the citizens by Emperor Friedrich III in 1481, were exercised only briefly. In 1511, Prince-Archbishop Leonhard von Keutschach put an end to this freedom in a highly aggressive coup, forcing the citizens to relinquish the imperial council prerogatives.

27 Zillner, *Geschichte I.*, p 430.

28 Ebd., II., p 697. – Cf. also Kramml, *Das Rathaus*, p 16.

29 Hübner, *Beschreibung*, vol. 2, p 435 f.

30 Lipburger, *Das sogenannte Cristan Reuttersche Stadtbuch*.

31 Spechtler/Uminsky, *Stadt- und Polizeiordnung*.

32 Ebd., p 185 f.

33 Cf. ebd., p 193 f.

34 Ebd. p 187.

35 E.g. in an order given on 12 August 1555 (AStS, town council protocols, 1555).

36 AStS, town council protocol, 1564, 20 March 1564, & AStS, town council protocol,1588, 15 Sept. 1588.

37 AStS, town council protocol, 1589, 13 Sept. 1589; cf. also ebd., 17 Sept. 1582, o. P.: obligation to provide the governor by 7 p.m. with a written register of all arrivals.

38 The original edict, a successfully restored, large-format parchment, is kept in the AStS, central archive 833; two 18th-century copies with slightly different wording are in the SLA, privy archive XXXV/Generale 1595/06/01.

39 Some of the names can be assigned to breweries: Georg Stöllner – Kasererbräu, Caspar Gatterer – Stieglbräu, Albrecht Graf – Steinbräu, Michael Holzhauser – Gablerbräu, Ruep Schiferl – Schlammbräu, Hanns Talhamer – Moserbräu, Hanns Holtzhäuser– Stockhamerbräu, Sebastian Seiller – Mödlhamerbräu, Hanns Schreiner – Bergerbräu. For the (later so named) Sternbrauerei, the sources give no name.

40 The period of three months to seek other employment was granted only to those who had many children or were poverty-stricken or otherwise without means of sustenance.

41 AStS, Pezoltakten 146, Umgeldmandat 1587; cf. Ammerer, *Steuer- und Finanzpolitik*, p 133, & Macht und Herrschaft, p 107 f.

42 On the many standardisation measures dictated by the Archbishop cf. Lobenwein, *Ordungen und Mandate*.

43 AStS, town council protocols, 1620, 8 May 1620, p 154.

From the Thiry Year's War to the beginning of the 18th century

1 Cf. Ammerer/Waitzbauer, *Wege zum Bier*, p 19.

2 Cf. Kreibich, *Hofbrauereien*, p 554.

3 In order to simplify calculation of the beverage levy, the various measures of capacity hitherto used in the archbishopric were standardised in 1666. From then on there was no longer the "short bucket" of 36 quarts, but only the "long bucket" of 40 quarts (1 quart = 1.57 litres).

4 AStS, ZA 855/1, no. 43, *notice to each and every official of the Archbishopric*, 18 February 1636.

5 Cf. Ammerer, *Macht und Herrschaft*, p 109.

6 SLA, privy archive XXVII/15: *Neue Steurbeschreibung der Hochfrst. Haubtstatt Salzburg de Anno 1632*, p 11. – That year's total tax in the Getreidegasse was 259,780 gulden, and in the whole town 1,392,310 gulden.

7 Cf. Wallentin, *Santino Solari*, p 314.

8 AStS, *Gemainer Statt Salzburg Zins und gilten buech* 1639.

9 AStS, BU 259, *Grundbuch der Stadt Salzburg*. 1650.

10 According to AStS, building documentation, Getreidegasse 34, *Sternbräu*

11 This date is apparent from the tax registers; cf. SLA, Doppler-Chronik 351. a.

12 AStS, BU 259, *Grundbuch der Stadt Salzburg*. 1650.

13 Cf. ibid.

14 Cf. SLA, Doppler-Chronik 351. 6; quoted after the *Kaufrechtsnotl* [land register].

15 The Stockhamer family brewed beer here from 1639 to 1744. In 1746 the business, together with the house at no. 35, passed to the Flatscher family. The *Stockhamerbräu* closed down in 1865.

16 Cf. Kreibich, *Hofbrauereien*, p 44.

17 Cf. Spatzenegger, *Blaue Gans*, p 29.

18 Cf. Ebner/Weigl, *Das Salzburger Wasser*, p 53.

19 Ibid.

20 AStS, BU 258, *Gemainer Statt Salzburg Zinß: vnd Giltenbuech* 1639, S. 59.

21 Ibid., p 69

22 SLA, HK, Umgeldamt Salzburg 1700 Q.

23 Cf. ibid.

24 Cf. Lipburger, *Stadtrecht*, p 54; Dopsch/Lipburger, *Das 16. Jahrhundert*, p 2055.

25 *Preuer vnd Prukhnechten Ordnung alhir zu Hällein*, Hallein town archives, 1592.

26 AStS, ZA 723, Handwerksordnung von 1625, Art. 13; cf. also Kreibich, *Hofbrauereien*, p 15.

27 This contained candles, the guild cross, documents, protocols, journeyman's books and other important papers and certificates.

28 AStS, ZA 855/1, no. 24, Handwerksordnung, undated

29 AStS, ZA 855/1, Nr. 36, notice from the guild of brewers and maltsers to the Archbishop on May 1645 concerning the guild's forthcoming *Jahrtag* on 26 June 1645.

30 AStS, ZA 723: §2 of the 1627 trade regulations for the brewers prescribed the adoption of a hostelry belonging *to an honest citizen or host*.

31 The trade's most important concerns could not be legally effectuated until the guild chest was opened.

32 AStS, ZA 422, brewers' apprentice ordinance.

33 AStS, ZA 855/12, no. 868, bill from the St. Johann Hospital, dated 4 June 1805, costs for medicine and board, 11 florins, 47 kronen, for the brewer's labourer Joseph Gerschweiler.

34 On these and other occasions, the tradesmen used special guild dishes; the drinking-vessels, mugs, tankards, jars and jugs, in particular, had specific ritual meanings.

35 AStS, ZA 855/4, no. 139, bill from the brewer Hans Adam Stockhamer, dated 7 June 1712.

36 Ibid., Nr. 334, bill dated 12 July 1740.

37 AStS, ZA 855/1, no. 28.

38 Quoted after Breitinger/Weinkammer/Dohle, *Handwerker*, p 327.

39 SLA, HK Salzburg/Stadtgericht 1676 C, letter from Georg Ehrenreich Stockhamer to the Archbishop, undated

40 According to the note to the Court Chamber on Stockhamer's letter, dated 30 August.

41 Letter from Christoph Egedacher, undated, dealt with by the Court Chamber on 27 September 1675.

42 SLA, HK Salzburg/Stadtgericht 1676 C, reply from Georg Ehrenreich Stockhamer, undated (1675).

43 Protocol of the court treasury, 19 February, concerning a letter from Egedacher dated 27 January 1675.

44 AStS, ZA 855/4, no. 124. – After a petition by the brewers, due to the price increase for barley a higher beer tariff was fixed at 5 kronen per quart (letter from the Court Chamber, dated 6 October 1692).

45 Cf. Weidenholzer, *Das Höllbräu*, p 74.

The many aspects of the Sternbräu. The 18th century

1 On the demographic development cf. Dopsch/Hoffmann, *Geschichte*, p 403–408.

2 Cf. Rau, *Orte der Gastlichkeit*, p 403; Scheutz, *Gaststätten*, pp 170–172; Fischer, *Bühnen und Spielplätze*, p 223 f.

3 *Ein Paar Briefe*, p 362.

4 Hübner, *Beschreibung*, vol. 2, p 614 f.; further quotations from 18th-century travel writers in Ammerer/Waitzbauer, *Wirtshäuser*, p 41.

5 ,SLA, Stadtsyndikat Nr. 1160, inventory of 7 April 1756.

6 Cf. Ammerer/Weiss, *Die Reise nach Salzburg*, p 15. – Leaving the town, one could take the 6 p.m. Thursday coach (alternately to Upper and Lower Austria, or Tyrol and Italy), the Friday 2 p.m. (to Lungau, Carinthia and on towards Trieste) or the Sunday 8 a.m. (to Munich, Regensburg, Nuremberg, etc.).

7 *Salzburger Intelligenzblatt XIX.*, 8 May 1790, col. 303.

8 Cf. AStS, Stadtratsprotokoll v. 1741, p 308 f., entry for 2 June 1741.

9 SLA, Geheimes Archiv XXV, *Gandt-Urtl. Johann Georgen Stockhamber gewest burgl. Würth, und Gastgeben, auch Pierpreuens beÿ dem sogenant guldenen Stern alhier, Credit-Weesen betr.*

10 AStS, Stadtratsprotokoll 1743, p 474 & pp 489–492 (4 Sept. 1743).

11 AStS, Pezolt Akten 362, Mathias Wilhemseder questioned at the Court Chamber, 1764, pag. 824; Weidenholzer, Zum Stern, p 546 f.; AStS, Pezolt-Akten 362, p 824.

12 The following according to George, *Familie Wilhelmseder*, pp 203–206.

13 Angermüller, *Antretter*, p 14.

14 Cf . George, *Familie Wilhelmseder*, p 212.

15 Cf. ibid., p 212.

16 AStS, ZA 855/7, no. 373, copy of an official request for an assessment following Johann Mathias Wilhelmseder's application for citizenship, dated 2 Dec. 1741.

17 AStS, Pezolt Akten 362, p 825.

18 AStS, Stadtratsprotokoll, 18 January 1742, p 18; George, *Familie Wilhelmseder*, p 214.

19 Cf. list in: Ammerer, Die frühe Neuzeit, p 136.

20 AStS, ZA 723: §2 of the 1627 trade regulations for the brewers prescribed the adoption of a hostelry belonging to an *honest citizen or host.*

21 Normative regulations for the journeymen's confraternity, cf. in AStS, ZA 721: *Vorhalt denen Lehr=Jungen vnd denen Borgen so Einer einen Aũfdingt oder Freÿsaget aũch wie man sich In denen Processionen vnd begröbnüssen zu verhalten hat.*

22 AStS, PA 1.161/1, e.g. 11 July 1774.

23 AStS, PA 1.161/2, 13 July 1790.

24 AStS, ZA 855/7, no. 373 (Letter from Johann Mathias Wilhelmseder applying for an apprenticeship, undated); similarly AStS, ZA 855/1, no. 25. – Cf. Ammerer/Baumgartner, Die Getreidegasse, p 45.

25 AStS, ZA 855/7, Nr. 373, memorandum from the municipal adminstration to the court councillor, undated.

26 The following according to: AStS, ZA 855/10, no. 531.

27 If an apprentice "ran away", the entire deposit went into the guild chest. If, on the other hand, he "committed a sin of the flesh" and fathered a child, the apprenticeship would be considered null and void. This entailed not only exclusion from the trade, but also to the forfeit of the 32 gulden pledge; cf. ibid., no. 580, & AStS, ZA 723, Handwerksordnung von 1625, Zi 6, 7 & 11.

28 AStS, ZA 723, Handwerksordnung von 1625, Zi 25.

29 AStS, Stadtratsprotokoll 1743, p 573 f.

30 Ibid., p 615 f.

31 AStS, ZA 855/7, no. 373, joint statement from all Salzburg landlords and brewers, undated.

32 Ibid., statement by the Salzburg town council, 22 Oct. 1743.

33 AStS, ZA 855/1, no. 25.

34 Ibid., p 641: *Ist sowohl dem gesambten Handtwerch, als auch dem Wilhelmseder in pleno fürgehalten worden.*

35 Cf. *Salzburg zur Zeit der Mozarts*, p 90.

36 SLA, Geheimes Archiv XXIII/24 ½. – Cf.: Mühlbacher, *Die Residenz*, p 54 f.

37 The following statements and figures according to SLA, Stadtsyndikat no. 1160, inventory of 7 April 1756.

38 Klehr, *Die Getreidegasse*, p 198.

39 Josef Eder, *Das alte Sternbräu-Haus*, in: Salzburger Volksblatt, 23 May 1925, p 3.

40 Cf. ÖKT XIII, p 262 f.

41 Cf. Brückler, *Franz Ferdinand*, p 500.

42 *Salzburg und Umgebung*, p 6. – Josef Eder, *Das alte Sternbräu-Haus*, in: *Salzburger Volksblatt*, 23 May 1925, p 3. – The only remark concerning the altar painting was that it had greatly darkened. In March 1930 the *Salzburger Chronik* reported its "rescue": Salzburg artist and restorer Christine Poeschl had remounted the badly deteriorated painting (executed by an anonymous though not first-rate artist, as was twice emphasised in this brief article), removed the layers of varnish and retouched the damaged patches, thus saving it from total decay; cf. *Restauriertes altes Gemälde*, in: *Salzburger Chronik* no. 56, 8 March 1930, p 9.

43 Cf. 1914 correspondence between the Sternbrau AG, the Conservation Authority and the imperial and royal Central Commission for the Preservation of Monuments in Vienna: Bundesdenkmalamt, Karton Salzburg-Stadt, Getreidegasse 34.

44 Wagner, *Die erste Barockisierung*, p 641.

45 The following according to ibid., p 638.

46 AStS, Pezolt Akten 362, pag. 890.

47 Bauer/Deutsch, Mozart. *Briefe und Aufzeichnungen*, 232/22 f.

48 All figures according to charts in SLA, Hofrat-Akten, Salzburg 104.

49 SLA, Hofrat-Akten, Salzburg 104, 1794 census.

50 For localisation cf. Ammerer/Waitzbauer, *Wirtshäuser*, end-paper.

51 Only after he moved to Vienna in 1780 do we learn about Mozart's beer-drinking habits; cf. e.g. Bauer/Deutsch, *Mozart. Briefe und Aufzeichnungen*, 697/33–46 (Wolfgang Amadeus Mozart to Martha Elisabeth Baronin von Waldstätten, Vienna, 2 Oct. 1782).

52 Cf. Ammerer/Waitzbauer, *Wirtshäuser*.

53 Bauer/Deutsch, *Mozart. Briefe und Aufzeichnungen*, 764/24 f., entry in Maria Anna Mozart's diary, 2 August 1783.

54 Bauer/Deutsch, Mozart. *Briefe und Aufzeichnungen*, 354/24 f. – The reference to family letters showing that Wolfgang Mozart enjoyed dancing with pretty Salzburg girls in the Sternbräu (Kernmayr, *Brot und Eisen*, p 339), may well originate in the author's imagination rather than a genuine source.

55 Cf. Breitinger, *Mundbäckentochter*.

56 The following statements are based on the survey of July 1764.

57 Ibid., p 844.

58 Ibid., 928, unpaged (after paging 940).

59 Ibid., paged, p 826.

60 Cf. Ammerer, *Hungersnot*.

61 Cf. Kreibich, *Salzburger Hofbrauereien*, p 297.

62 Cf. ibid.

63 Cf. Zillner, *Geschichte der Stadt Salzburg* 2/2, pp 369 & 373.

64 Weidenholzer, *Zum Stern*, p 547.

65 AStS, Stadtratsprotokoll 1772, p 105 f.

66 Ibid., p 288 f. – Lat.: licitari = to bid at an auction.

67 Ibid., p 289.

68 Ibid., p 290.

69 Ibid., p 301.

70 AStS, BU, Stadtratsprotokoll for 1772, p 21.

71 Ibid., p 104.

72 Stadtarchiv Tittmoning, Fach 161/1, Götz von Dobenek, Urkunden; AStS, Stadtratsprotokoll 1772, p 21. – After he had received permission for the transfer of those items, he wrote a letter of thanks to the town council. – Johann Mathias Wilhelmseder died on 16 April 1801 and was buried in the Bürgerspital cemetery in Salzburg. The grave slab is in the Hospital Church of St. Blasius.

73 Cf. Angermüller, *Antretter von Antrettern*, p 13.

74 On the question of the occasion cf. ibid. p. 14.

75 Cf. Klein, *Bevölkerung und Siedlung*, p 1308.

76 Statistics for the 1790s even show a ratio of c. 3:2; cf. Ammerer, *Hungersnot*, p 192.

77 *Preise der Lebensmittel. Diese Preise sind seit wenigen Jahren außerordentlich gestiegen, und bey einigen Lebensbedürfnissen z. B. Brod, Mehl ec, beynahe über ein Drittel angewachsen* (Hübner, *Beschreibung*, vol. 2, p 425).

78 Cit. from Angermüller, *Antretter von Antrettern*, p 13.

79 AStS, Protokoll des Stadtrats, 9 March 1746.

80 AStS, *General Geföhl Buech … 1742*, p 547.

81 The *Bierumgelds=Ordnung* of 23 Aug. 1774 is published in: Zauner, *Auszug der wichtigsten hochfürstl. Salzburgischen Landesgesetze*, vol. 2, Salzburg 1787, pp 31–34.

82 Cf. Hübner, *Beschreibung*, vol. 2, p 454. – The repeal of the excise was announced in the *Salzburger Intelligenzblatt*. The reason given was that the state finances were back in order: … *dass Einnahme und Ausgabe Unsers Reichsfürstenthumes ein ersprießliches Gleichverhältnis errungen zu haben scheinen* (Salzburger Intelligenzblatt XLII., 17 Oct. 1789, col. 655–657, quote col. 655).

83 Ibid., no. 578, letter from the brewers' guild master to the court councillor and the town syndic, dated 20 Dec. 1778.

84 Breitinger/Weinkammer/Dohle, *Handwerker*, p 328 f.

85 SLA, Hieronymus-Kataster, fol. 1078.

86 Also: Böstlin; cf. SLA, Doppler-Chronik, printed: p 376.

87 Hübner, *Beschreibung*, vol. 1, p 31.

88 Cf. chart 2 in Klein, *Bevölkerung und Siedlung*, p 1343 (1795: 16,837 persons in the town's parishes; 1805: 16,060).

89 Ammerer, *Das Kaffeehaus*, p 180.

90 In the original: *Si le bon Dieu ne met fin à tous ses désordres en nous accordant la paix, nous pouvons nous attendre à être chassé d'un après l'autre non pas par l'ennemie, mais par nos propres sujets* (Státní Archiv v Zámrsku, RA Colloredo-Mansfeld, Kart. 61, fol. 556ʳ, letter of 18 Febr. 1795).

91 Universitätsarchiv Salzburg, Fasz. 59 a no. 23 a (letter from the municipal judge to the rector of Salzburg University, 9 February 1798).

92 Ibid., six-page printed decree by the Archbishop, 1 July 1800. Not until 6 May 1801 did an order from the interim governorship extend closing time again by one hour.

93 Cf. Hammermayer, *Die letzte Epoche*, pp 502–515.

94 Cf. in detail: Ammerer/Weiss, *Die Säkularisation Salzburgs*.

95 AStS, Pezolt-Akten 157, *Tabellarische Uebersicht Aller Gebäude der Hauptstadt Salzburg samt den zweÿ Vorstädten. Mülln, und Nonnthal …"* (1802).

96 SLA, Landschaft VII/37, letter from the court council, 20 June 1791 (Franz Thaddäus von Kleinmayrn & Philip Gäng) & for the *Landschaft* Franz Staiger, 25 May 1791, with statements from the neighbours.

97 The following acc. AStS, Pezolt-Akten 224.

98 *Augenscheins-Protokoll*, 2 November 1804.

99 Franz Leonhard Lämmer, administrator of the Buchdruckermayer-Haus am unteren Gries no. 115, Christian Greibl, barber-surgeon, house no. 19, Math. Kaut, baker, for houses nos. 74 and 73, Math. Maÿr, grocer, for house no. 75, Joh. Wisser, master shoemaker, for house no. 76 and Caspar Schmid, gardener and shop-owner.

100 *Wandscheiben* was the version of bowling where the ball had first to touch the side wall of the alley before reaching the pins – which required great skill. This version was also played at the major public bowling competitions in the *Stieglbräu* garden (cf. Ammerer/Waitzbauer, *Wirtshäuser*, p 73).

From one-man business to public limited company

1 Cf. Preiss, *Hofbrauhaus.*

2 Cf. Mösenlechner, *Firmengeschichte.*

3 Cf. Hinterseer, *Heimat-Chronik Lofer-St. Martin.*

4 Cf. Ammerer/Waitzbauer, *Wege zum Bier.*

5 Cf. Hoffmann, Salzburg.

6 *Amts- und Intelligenz-Blatt zur kaiserl. königl. privilegirten Salzburger Zeitung*, 1 October 1832, p 1281 f.

7 *Amts- und Intelligenz-Blatt zur kaiserl. königl. privilegirten Salzburger Zeitung*, 2 November 1832, p 1437 f.

8 Grave slab in St. Sebastian's cemetery: "Denkmahl des Herrn Georg Ellinger, Pächter des Sternbräuhauses allhier…" [memorial to Herr Georg Ellinger, lessee of the Sternbräu house here...]

9 Cf. Ammerer/Waitzbauer, *Wirtshäuser.*

10 Cf. Schwarz, *Besucher Salzburgs.*

11 *Kaiserl. Koenigl. Oesterreichisches Amts- und Intelligenzblatt von Salzburg*, 21 February 1825, p 256.

12 SM, poster collection

13 Ibid.

14 Weilmeyr, *Salzburg*, p 306.

15 Ibid., p 307

16 Cf. AStS, NStA fasc. 170b no. 6, letter no. 6223 from the Provincial government to the municipal council in Salzburg, 31 May 1858.

17 AStS, NStA fasc. 175a, building application from Anton Hörl, 31 May 1 862.

18 AStS, NStA fasc. 176, protocol of on-site inspection, 23 April 1863.

19 *Stieglkeller und Sterngarten vor 70 Jahren*, in: *Salzburger Volksblatt*, 19 May 1934.

20 Ibid.

21 SM, poster *Vorversammlung*, 8 December 1871.

22 Cf. Ammerer/Waitzbauer, *Wege zum Bier*, esp. pp 59–65.

23 SLA, Grundbuch Salzburg Innere Stadt, EZ 360, Getreidegasse 34–36.

24 AStS, BA, Getreidegasse 34–36.

25 *Salzburger Zeitung*, 5 July 1886, p 2.

26 SLA, Landesausschussakten III, Statuten der Aktiengesellschaft "Sternbräu" in Salzburg, Sonderfaszikel 74/10/01 betr. Sternbräu Aktiengesellschaft.

27 Cf. Mussoni, *Eisengewerkschaft*, p 1–32.

28 UBS, *Arbeits-Ordnung für die Brauerei Actiengesellschaft Sternbräu in Salzburg*. In effect from 1 July 1888.

29 Cf. RGBl. 22/1885, *Gesetz vom 8. März 1885, betreffend die Abänderung und Ergänzung der Gewerbeordnung*, pp 35–51.

30 UBS, *Arbeits-Ordnung für die Brauerei Actiengesellschaft Sternbräu in Salzburg*. In effect from 1 July 1888.

31 Ibid.

32 Cf. Ammerer/Waitzbauer, *Wege zum Bier*, esp. pp 59–65.

33 Cf. Hahnl/Hoffmann/Müller, *Stadtteil Riedenburg*, p 581.

34 AStS, Gewerbeakten XIV B 1, Sternbrauerei 1894, licence application, 2 July 1892.

35 Ibid.

36 Ibid.

37 Ibid.

38 *Salzburger Tagblatt*, 19 February 1902, p 1 f.

39 *Salzburger Tagblatt*, 13 September 1902, p 4.

40 *Salzburger Tagblatt*, 13 February 1903, p 4.

41 *Salzburger Volksblatt*, 6 July 1907, p 6.

42 *Salzburger Tagblatt*, 9 November 1906, p 3.

43 Ibid.

44 Schobersberger, *Baumeister einer Epoche*; p 723.

45 *Salzburger Volksblatt*, 6 July 1907, p 6.

46 *Salzburger Tagblatt*, 6 July 1907, p 5.

47 *Salzburger Volksblatt*, 17 February 1888.

48 *Salzburger Zeitung*, 17 May 1888.

49 Ibid.

50 Ibid.

51 Ibid.

52 Sternbräu Salzburg, unpaged.

53 Ibid., unpaged.

54 Ibid., unpaged.

55 Ibid., unpaged.

56 SM, calendar poster *Sternbrauerei Salzburg* 1909.

57 Jubilee edition of the *Salzburger Chronik*, 50 (1914), p 69.

58 *Salzburger Chronik*, 1 March 1909, p 9.

59 Jubilee edition of the *Salzburger Chronik*, 50 (1914), p 69.

60 Pflanzl, *Berta Pflanzl*, p 24.

61 Halbach, *Salzburg*, unpaged.

62 *Salzburg, Stadt und Land*, p 40.

63 *Salzburger Volksblatt*, 18 July 1910, p 13.

64 Cf. Kunz, *Monumentalbauten.*

65 Ibid., p 19.

66 Cäsar, *Gesamtbebauungsplan.*

Reconstruction and expansion, crises and wars. 1914–1945

1 Lackner, *Volksernährung*, p 8.
2 Cf. Weidenholzer, *Not*, p 64.
3 Hellmuth, *Acker und Wiesen*, p 51.
4 UBS, account rendered by the *Aktiengesellschaft Sternbräu* in Salzburg of the XXVIII fiscal year 1913/14 for the annual general meeting on Saturday 12 December 1914 at 10.30 a.m. at Steinbruchstrasse no. 1, ground floor right, in Salzburg.
5 UBS, account rendered by the *Aktiengesellschaft Sternbräu* in Salzburg of the XXXI fiscal year 1916/17 for the annual general meeting on Thursday 13 December 1917 at 10 a.m., at Steinbruchstrasse no. 1, ground floor right, in Salzburg.
6 *Salzburg von August 1916 bis August 1917*, in: *Ruperti-Kalender for 1918*, p 90.
7 Ibid.
8 Cf. Hanisch, *Alltag*, p 44.
9 *Salzburger Chronik*, 15 November 1916, p 3.
10 *Salzburger Chronik*, 15 April 1917, p 10.
11 Ibid.
12 *Salzburger Chronik*, 4 December 1917, p 5.
13 *Salzburger Chronik*, 11 October 1916, p 4; *Salzburger Chronik*, 10 January 1917, p 3; *Salzburger Chronik*, 11 April 1918, p 3.
14 *Salzburger Chronik*, 17 March 1917, p 4.
15 *Salzburger Chronik*, 10 August 1918, p 6.
16 *Salzburger Chronik*, 16 August 1918, p 5.
17 Ibid.
18 For further details, see Köfner, *Geschichte Salzburgs*.
19 *Salzburger Chronik*, 26 July 1918, p 3.
20 Ibid.
21 UBS, account rendered by the *Aktiengesellschaft Sternbräu* in Salzburg of the XXXII fiscal year 1917/18 for the annual general meeting on Thursday 12 December 1918 at 10 a.m., at Steinbuchstrasse no. 1, ground floor right, in Salzburg.
22 Grasmayr was originally a poor itinerant teacher who married a member of the Mautner-Markhof family; however, he remained all his life more of a litérateur, bon-vivant and eccentric.
23 AStS, BA Getreidegasse 34–36, letter from the Stadtbauamt Salzburg, 29 July 1921.
24 UBS, account rendered by the *Aktiengesellschaft Sternbräu* in Salzburg of the 35th fiscal year 1920/21 for the annual general meeting on Thursday 15 December 1921 at 10 a.m., at Steinbruchstrasse no. 1, ground floor right, in Salzburg.
25 SLA, letters from Rehrl, 1920/209, letter from Johann Zerdik to Franz Rehrl dated 4 May 1920.
26 Ibid., letter from Franz Rehrl to Johann Zerdik dated 21 May 1920.
27 AStS, BA Getreidegasse 34, letter from the building authority to the folk theatre society "D'Kreuzlschreiber2, 21 February 1925.
28 AStS, BA Getreidegasse 34, technical report, 11 December 1923.
29 AStS, BA Getreidegasse 34, letter from the building authority to the folk theatre society "D'Kreuzlschreiber", 21 February 1925.
30 *Salzburger Volksblatt*, 7 December 1923, p 4.
31 Further details in Ammerer/Waitzbauer, *Wirtshäuser*, pp 151–154.
32 *Salzburger Volksblatt*, 28 June 1926, p 7.
33 *Salzburger Chronik*, 19 April 1927, p 4.
34 Paul Stefan, *Festspielstadt Salzburg*, in: *Die Stunde*, 29 July 1928.
35 *Salzburger Volksblatt*, 21 March 1928, p 6.
36 SLA, Grundbuch Salzburg Innere Stadt, EZ 360, Getreidegasse 34–36.
37 UBS, account rendered by the *Aktiengesellschaft Sternbräu* in Salzburg of the 39th fiscal year 1924/25 for the annual general meeting on Thursday 10 December 1925, at 10 a.m. at Steinbruchstrasse no. 1, ground floor right, in Salzburg.
38 *Salzburger Volksblatt*, 23 September 1926.
39 *Salzburger Chronik*, 23 September 1926, p 6.
40 Ibid., p 10.
41 Ibid., p 6.
42 BDA, Karton Salzburg-Stadt, Griesgasse 21–39, letter from the Salzburg town council to the Sternbräu AG, dated 20 October 1926.
43 Ibid.
44 BDA, Karton Salzburg-Stadt, Griesgasse 21–39, file memorandum of the K. k. Landes-Denkmalamt Salzburg [office for the protection of historical monuments...!], dated 10 May 1927.
45 ÖKT XIII, p 282 f.; Frank, *Mönchsberg*, p 38.
46 *Salzburger Volksblatt*, 23 September 1926.
47 *Salzburger Volksblatt*, 18 September 1926, p 16.
48 *Führer durch Salzburg*, p 9.
49 *Salzburger Volksblatt*, 17 August 1929, p 8.
50 Sungler, *Bürgerstuben*, p 26.
51 Haller, *Das Neosgraffito*, p 1.
52 Cf. Ibid.
53 *Salzburger Volksblatt*, 26 June 1929, p 9.
54 SLA, Grundbuch Salzburg, Innere Stadt, EZ 360, Getreidegasse 34–36.
55 Friedl, *Salzburger Brauereiindustrie*, p 90.
56 *50 Jahre Österreichische Brau-Aktiengesellschaft*, p 6.
57 Cf. *Compass*. Financial year-book vol. 13, Vienna 1935, p 809.
58 *Salzburger Chronik*, 30 April 1931, p 3.
59 AStS, BA Getreidegasse 34–36, town council protocol concerning the application by the Sternbräu AG for permission to carry out alterations to the Sternbräu, Griesgasse 23, 27 February 1930.
60 *Salzburger Chronik*, 30 April 1931, p 3.
61 *Salzburger Chronik*, 11 December 1930, p 4.
62 *Salzburger Volksblatt*, 30 April 1931, p 5.
63 *Salzburger Chronik*, 30. April 1931, p 3.
64 Ibid., p 4.
65 Ibid.
66 Ibid.

67 Ibid.

68 Ibid.

69 Dopsch/Hoffmann, *Geschichte*, p 260 f.

70 AStS, BA, Getreidegasse 34–36, report by the Salzburg building authority, 29 July 1921.

71 Ibid.

72 AStS, BA, Getreidegasse 34–36, letter of complaint to the Salzburg police, 4 February 1930.

73 Ibid.

74 Ibid.

75 Ibid., letter from the police to the town council, 22 February 1930.

76 Ibid., report from police office Karl Walkner, Bundes-Sicherheitswache Salzburg, Wachtposten Rathaus, concerning the keeping of pigs, 22 June 1930.

77 Ibid., letter from the police department to the town council, 24 June 1930.

78 Ibid., Salzburg town council protocol concerning the keeping of pigs in the Sternbräu, 12 August 1930, p 1.

79 Ibid., p 6.

80 *Salzburger Volksblatt*, 1 September 1933, p 8.

81 Otruba, *A. Hitler's "Tausend-Mark-Sperre"*, p 117.

82 SLA, Rehrl-Briefe 1935/2945, letter from Emil Ludwig to Hans Hofmann-Montanus, 19 October 1935.

83 Ibid.

84 Ibid.

85 *Salzburger Volksblatt*, 5 January 1938, p 10.

86 *Salzburger Volksblatt*, 20 January 1938, p 8.

87 *Salzburger Volksblatt*, 31 January 1938, p 8.

88 Ibid.

89 Kraft durch Freude (KdF) [strength through joy]: an organisation of the German Labour Front (DAF), which provided affordable leisure activities and holidays in grand style to strengthen the "people's community" and promote public health.

90 Cf. Lichtblau, *In Lebensgefahr*, esp. pp 78–85.

91 *Salzburger Landeszeitung*, 10 November 1938.

92 Cf. Lichtblau, *In Lebensgefahr*, p 85.

93 Cf. Kerschbaumer, *Gausuppe*, p 216.

94 *Salzburger Volksblatt*, 23 December 1938, p 6.

95 Ibid.

96 Ibid.

97 Ibid.

98 *Salzburger Landeszeitung*, 2 February 1939, p 8.

99 *Salzburger Landeszeitung*, 25 May 1939, p 7.

100 *Salzburger Landeszeitung*, 26 September 1939, p 7.

101 *Salzburger Landeszeitung*, 20 November 1939, p 8.

102 Ibid.

103 Kerschbaumer, *Faszination*, p 279.

104 Archiv Kaltenhausen, Aktenordner Sternbräu, summary of the history of the Sternbräu, dated 2 December 1963.

105 Marx, *"Dann ging es Schlag auf Schlag"*, p 263.

106 Ibid.

107 Ibid., p 264.

On the road to the present day. 1945 to today

1 Bauer, *Welcome Ami*, p 147.

2 For further details, see Fasching/Rainer, *Dislokation*.

3 Cf. Ammerer, *Das Tomaselli*, pp 191–194.

4 AStS, Bauakten Getreidegasse 36/Griesgasse 23, Bauakt 1937, application for exemption from building ban, 15 October 1945.

5 Cf. Bauer, *Welcome Ami*, p 176.

6 Quoted from ibid., p 175.

7 *Salzburger Nachrichten*, 17 December 1945, p 3.

8 *Salzburger Nachrichten*, 29 May 1946, p 3.

9 *Salzburger Nachrichten*, 14. November 1947, p 3.

10 Ibid.

11 AStS, Gewerbeakten Ia3, Sternbräu Gasthof 1949, letter from Alois Schnöll to the town council, dated 31 March 1949.

12 AStS, Gewerbeakten Ia3, Sternbräu Gasthof 1949, official town council memorandum, 8 April 1949.

13 *Salzburger Nachrichten*, 1 October 1949, p 2.

14 Ibid.

15 *Demokratisches Volksblatt*, 1 October 1949, p 5.

16 *Demokratisches Volksblatt*, 29/30 July 1950, p 13.

17 Ibid.

18 Kaut, *Salzburg von A–Z*, p 74.

19 *Salzburger Nachrichten*, 14 October 1954, p 3.

20 *Salzburger Nachrichten*, 17 April 1954.

21 *Salzburger Nachrichten*, 16 March 1953, p 5.

22 http://www.wienerzeitung.at/nachrichten/wien/stadtleben/241456_Der-Sieg-des-Willens-ueber-den-Schmerz.html, article of 26 March 2009, accessed on 19 August 2014.

23 *Salzburger Nachrichten*, 10 November 1956, p 5.

24 AStS, pre-death estate of Harald Engländer (by kind permission of Peter F. Kramml, head of the Salzburg town archives).

25 Ibid.

26 Ibid.

27 Archiv Kaltenhausen, Aktenordner Sternbräu, letter from mayor Alfred Bäck to the board of direstors of the Brau AG, 2 November 1959.

28 Ibid., letter from the Österreichische Brau-Aktiengesellschaft to mayor Alfred Bäck, 12 November 1959.

29 Ibid.

30 Ibid., Bescheid Zl. VI/1 – 9590/59 des Magistrats Salzburg, 17 December 1959.

31 Ibid., press service of the Österreichische Brau AG, re: Grossgasthof Sternbräu erweitert, 30 December 1963.

32 Neureiter/Zwink, *Salzburg – wo?*, p 98 f.

33 Kobes, K+K+K, p 90.

34 Ibid., p 99.

35 AStS, Sign. 010.385, Österreichische Brau AG, Das Projekt „Vitalisierung Sternbräu", dated 27 February 1986.

36 Ibid.

37 Ibid.

38 *Salzburger Nachrichten*, 28 February 1986, p 7.

39 *Salzburger Tagblatt*, 28 February 1986, p 13.

40 *Neue Salzburg Krone*, 27 August 1986, p 1.

41 Ibid.

42 Cf. *Salzburger Nachrichten*, 28 February 1986, p 7.

43 Quoted from *Salzburger Nachrichten*, 10 June 1995, p 29.

44 http://search.salzburg.com/display/SNA17850-19980313, accessed on 24 August 2014.

45 Cf. http://derstandard.at/2064781, 3 June 2005, accessed on 24 August 2014.

46 http://www.echosalzburg.at/index.php?option=com_content&view=article&id=857:star-der-gastronomie&catid=32:wirtschaft&Itemid=62, 1 November 2008, accessed on 24 August 2014.

47 http://search.salzburg.com/display/ks071600_07.01.2013_41-44411730, SN (local news section), accessed on 26 August 2014.

48 Ibid.

Picture credits

Stefan Andriska: 133
Archiv der Stadt Salzburg: 22–25, 32, 34 left, 36, 38, 42, 47 right, 48, 53 f.,
60–62, 64 right, 67–69 left, 74, 75, 83 top, 96, 98, 99, 106 left, 109 bottom,
114, 115, 120, 124, 126, 129, 130 bottom
Archiv Residenzprojekt Salzburg/Hubert Auer: 20 f.
Authors: 10, 12 right, 27, 33, 45, 51 right, 84, 87 top, 107 top, 108 top,
111, 130 top, 131, 134 right, 138 bottom, middle
Bundesdenkmalamt: 11, 57 right, 101 left
Cosy-Verlag: 107 bottom, 108 bottom, 116
Erzabtei St. Peter: 30, 34 right, 56, 57
IBT/Alexander Lohmann: 9 bottom
IBT/Andreas Kolarik: 18
IBT/Erika Mayer: 6, 8, 12 left, 14, 17, 19, 21 right, 37, 41, 49, 101 right, 102 top,
104, 141, 142, 143, 144, 155 left
IBT/fmt-pictures: 9 top
Harald Kratzer: 118, 128, 132, 134 left, 135, 136, 137, 138 top, right, 139
Harald Kratzer/Wildbild: 140
Mozart-Archiv (Mozarteum Foundation): 59.
Christa Nolte-Freundsberger: 88, 102 bottom, 103
Reinbert Reichenbacher: 109 top
Salzburg Museum: 13, 26, 30, 35, 40, 44, 50 f., 52, 66, 69 right, 70, 73, 76,
82 left, 85 top, 86, 87 bottom, 100 bottom, 106 right, 117, 127 left
Salzburger Landesarchiv: 39, 63, 64 f., 78 bottom, 82 right, 97, 105, 113 right
Stieglbrauerei zu Salzburg: 5, 80, 92, 112, 113 left
Stieglbrauerei zu Salzburg/Michael Mauracher: 50 left
Universitätsbibliothek Salzburg: 28, 29, 46, 47 left, 78 top, 79
Verlag Anton Pustet/Tanja Kühnel: 43, 72

Abbreviations

AStS	= Archiv der Stadt Salzburg	[town archives]
BA	= Bauakten	[building documents]
BDA	= Bundesdenkmalamt	[Federal Monuments Office]
EZ	= Einlagezahl	[entry number]
HK	= Hofkammer	[court chamber]
LG	= Landesgericht	[regional court]
MGSL	= Mitteilungen der Gesellschaft für Salzburger Landeskunde [notices from the Society for Regional and Cultural Studies]	
NStA	= Neuere Städtische Akten	[municipal records]
ÖKT	= Österreichische Kunsttopographie	[Austrian art topography]
RGBl.	= Reichsgesetzblatt	[Reich Law Gazette]
SLA	= Salzburger Landesarchiv	[Province of Salzburg archives]
SM	= Salzburg Museum	
STG	= Strafgesetzbuch	[criminal code]
UBS	= Universitätsbibliothek Salzburg	[University library]
ZA	= Zunftarchiv	[guild archive]

List of references

50 Jahre Österreichische Brau-Aktiengesellschaft = 50 Jahre Österreichische Brau-Aktiengesellschaft 1921–1971, hg. von der Österreichischen Brau-Aktiengesellschaft, zusammengestellt von Dipl. Ing. Georg Beurle, Linz 1971.

Ammerer, Das Kaffeehaus = Gerhard Ammerer, Das Kaffeehaus. Ort des Gesprächs, des Streites, des Spiels, der Lektüre und des Konsums, in: Ders./Weidenholzer, Rathaus – Kirche – Wirt, S. 157–167.

Ammerer, Das Tomaselli = Gerhard Ammerer, Das Tomaselli und die Salzburger Kaffeehaustradition seit 1700, Wien 2006.

Ammerer, Die frühe Neuzeit = Ammerer, Die frühe Neuzeit. Von Wolf Dietrich bis zur Säkularisation, in: Ders./Heinz Dopsch (Red.), Chronik der Salzburger Wirtschaft, Salzburg 1988, ²1991, S. 126–151.

Ammerer, Hungersnot = Gerhard Ammerer, Hungersnot, in: Ders./Angermüller, Das Salzburger Mozart-Lexikon, S. 192.

Ammerer, Macht und Herrschaft = Gerhard Ammerer, Macht und Herrschaft – Politik, Souveränitätsanspruch und Steuerstaat, in: Ders., Ingonda Hannesschläger (Hg.), Strategien der Macht. Hof und Residenz in Salzburg um 1600 – Architektur, Repräsentation und Verwaltung unter Fürsterzbischof Wolf Dietrich von Raitenau 1587 bis 1611/12, 28. Ergänzungsbd. der MGSL, Salzburg 2011, S. 85–118.

Ammerer, Steuer- und Finanzpolitik = Gerhard Ammerer, Zur Steuer- und Finanzpolitik Wolf Dietrichs von Raitenau (1587–1612), in: Salzburg-Archiv 2 (1986), S. 131–146.

Ammerer/Angermüller, Das Salzburger Mozart-Lexikon = Gerhard Ammerer, Rudolph Angermüller (Red.), Das Salzburger Mozart-Lexikon, hg. v. Land Salzburg und der Internationalen Salzburg Association, Bad Honnef 2005.

Ammerer/Baumgartner, Die Getreidegasse = Gerhard Ammerer, Jutta Baumgartner, Die Getreidegasse. Salzburgs berühmteste Straße, ihre Häuser, Geschäfte und Menschen, Salzburg 2011, ²2013.

Ammerer/Waitzbauer, Wege zum Bier = Gerhard Ammerer, Harald Waitzbauer: Wege zum Bier. 600 Jahre Braukultur. Mit Spaziergängen durch die Stadt Salzburg und Ausflügen in die Umgebung (Schriftenreihe des Archivs der Stadt Salzburg 32; Salzburg Studien. Forschungen zur Geschichte, Kunst und Kultur 11), Salzburg 2011.

Ammerer/Waitzbauer, Wirtshäuser = Gerhard Ammerer, Harald Waitzbauer. Wirtshäuser. Eine Kulturgeschichte der Salzburger Gaststätten, Salzburg 2014.

Ammerer/Weidenholzer, Rathaus – Kirche – Wirt = Gerhard Ammerer, Thomas Weidenholzer (Hg.), Rathaus – Kirche – Wirt. Öffentliche Räume in der Stadt Salzburg (Schriftenreihe des Archivs der Stadt Salzburg 26), Salzburg 2009.

Ammerer/Weiß, Die Reise nach Salzburg = Gerhard Ammerer und Alfred Stefan Weiß, Die Reise nach Salzburg, in: Gerhard Ammerer, Peter Kramml, Sabine Veits-Falk, Alfred Stefan Weiß, ReiseStadt Salzburg. Salzburg in der Reiseliteratur vom Humanismus bis zum beginnenden Eisenbahnzeitalter (Schriftenreihe des Archivs der Stadt Salzburg 17), Salzburg 2003, S. 7–24.

Ammerer/Weiß, Die Säkularisation Salzburgs = Gerhard Ammerer, Alfred Stefan Weiß (Hg.), Die Säkularisation Salzburgs 1803. Voraussetzungen – Ereignisse – Folgen (Veröffentlichungen des Internationalen Forschungszentrums für Grundfragen der Wissenschaften Salzburg Band 11), Frankfurt am Main 2005.

Angermüller, Antretter = Rudolph Angermüller, Antretter von Antrettern, in: Ammerer/ders., Das Salzburger Mozart-Lexikon, S. 12–15.

Bauer, Welcome Ami = Ingrid Bauer, Welcome Ami Go Home. Die amerikanische Besatzung in Salzburg 1945–1955, Erinnerungslandschaften aus einem Oral-History-Projekt, Salzburg-München 1998.

Bauer/Deutsch, Mozart. Briefe und Aufzeichnungen = Mozart. Briefe und Aufzeichnungen. Gesamtausgabe, hg. v. der Internationalen Stiftung Mozarteum Salzburg. Gesammelt und erläutert von Wilhelm A. Bauer und Otto Erich Deutsch, Kassel 1962–75; Bände I–IV Text, Bände V und VI Kommentar, auf Grund deren Vorarbeiten erläutert von Joseph Heinz Eibl; zitiert nach Brief- und Zeilennummer(n).

Breitinger, Mundbäckentochter = Friedrich Breitinger, Mozart und die „großaugerte Mundbäckentocher", in: Friederike Prodinger, Josef Brettenthaler (Hg.), Mozartiana „Gaulimauli Malefishu". Erhebungen von Friedrich Breitinger, Salzburg 1992, S. 160–164.

Brückler, Franz Ferdinand = Theodor Brückler, Thronfolger Franz Ferdinand als Denkmalschützer. Die „Kunstakten" der Militärkanzlei im Österreichischen Staatsarchiv (Kriegsarchiv) (Studien zu Denkmalschutz und Denkmalpflege XX), Wien-Köln-Weimar 2009.

Cäsar, Gesamtbebauungsplan = Martin Cäsar, Gesamtbebauungsplan der Stadt Salzburg, Diss. an der Technischen Hochschule Wien, Wien 1933.

Dopsch/Hoffmann, Geschichte = Heinz Dopsch, Robert Hoffmann, Geschichte der Stadt Salzburg, Salzburg–München 1996.

Dopsch/Lipburger, Das 16. Jahrhundert = Heinz Dopsch, Peter M. Lipburger, Das 16. Jahrhundert – von Leonhard von Keutschach zu Wolf Dietrich von Raitenau (1519–1587), in: Heinz Dopsch, Hans Spatzenegger (Hg.), Geschichte Salzburgs. Stadt und Land, II/4. Teil, Salzburg 1991, S. 2015–2070.

Ebner/Weigl, Das Salzburger Wasser = Romana Ebner, Herbert Weigl, Das Salzburger Wasser. Geschichte der Wasserversorgung der Stadt Salzburg. Mit einem Vorwort von Reinhold Reith (Schriftenreihe des Archivs der Stadt Salzburg 39), Salzburg 2014.

Ein Paar Briefe = Ein Paar Briefe über Salzburg, in: Der Weltbürger: oder deutsche Annalen der Menschheit und Unmenschheit, der Aufklärung und Unaufgeklärtheit, der Sittlichkeit und Unsittlichkeit 3 (1792) H. 7, S. 362.

Fasching/Rainer, Dislokation = Gerhard L. Fasching, Otto H. Rainer, Die Dislokation der US-Streitkräfte 1945 bis 1955 in Salzburg, in: Salzburg 1945–1955, Zerstörung und Wiederaufbau (Jahresschrift des Salzburger Museums Carolino Augusteum 40/41), Salzburg 1995, S. 289–321.

Fischer, Bühnen und Spielplätze = Friedrich J. Fischer, Bühnen und Spielplätze in der Stadt Salzburg im 18. Jahrhundert, in: Jahresschrift des Salzburger Museum Carolino Augusteum 5, Salzburg 1959, S. 223–238.

Frank, Mönchsberg = Adolf Frank, Der Mönchsberg und seine Baulichkeiten, in: MGSL 70 (1930), S. 1–44.

Friedl, Salzburger Brauereiindustrie = Klaus Friedl, Die Salzburger Brauereiindustrie in den letzten hundert Jahren unter besonderer Berücksichtigung des Halleiner Raumes (Kaltenhausen), Dipl.arbeit, Linz 1973.

Führer durch Salzburg = Ludwig Purtschellers großer Führer durch Salzburg – Stadt und Land, 31. Auflage, Salzburg 1927.

George, Familie Wilhelmseder = Dieter George, Die Tittmoninger Familie Wilhelmseder und ihre Verbindung nach Salzburg, in: Salzfass. Heimatkundliche Zeitschrift des Historischen Vereins Rupertiwinkel e. V., 43. Jg., Heft 2 (2009), S. 197–227.

Gierse, Tagebuch = Ludwig Gierse, Das Salzburger Tagebuch des Malers Friedrich Baudri aus dem Jahre 1836, in: MGSL 117 (1977), S. 269–370.

Hahnl/Hoffmann/Müller, Stadtteil Riedenburg = Adolf Hahnl, Robert Hoffmann, Guido Müller, Der Stadtteil Riedenburg. Bau- und Entwicklungsgeschichte bis 1945, in: MGSL 126 (1986), S. 569–584.

Halbach, Salzburg = Leon Halbach, Salzburg und Umgebung, Salzburg 1897.

Haller, Das Neosgraffito = Christian Haller, Das Neosgraffito von Karl Reisenbichler unter dem Aspekt seiner Erd- und Volksverbundenheit, phil. Diss., Salzburg 1991.

Hammermayer, Die letzte Epoche = Ludwig Hammermayer, Die letzte Epoche des Erzstifts Salzburg. Politik und Kirchenpolitik unter Erzbischof Graf Hieronymus Colloredo (1772–1803), in: Heinz Dopsch, Hans Spatzenegger (Hg.), Geschichte Salzburgs. Stadt und Land, II/1, Salzburg 1988, S. 453–535.

Hanisch, Alltag = Ernst Hanisch, Alltag im Krieg, in: Oskar Dohle, Thomas Mitterecker (Hg.), Salzburg im Ersten Weltkrieg. Fernab der Front – dennoch im Krieg (Schriftenreihe des Forschungsinstitutes für politische-historische Studien der Dr.-Wilfried-Haslauer-Bibliothek, Salzburg Band 48; Schriftenreihe des Archivs der Erzdiözese Salzburg 13; Schriftenreihe des Salzburger Landesarchivs Nr. 22), Wien-Köln-Weimar 2014, S. 33–45.

Hauthaler/Martin, Salzburger Urkundenbuch I und II = Willibald Hauthaler, Franz Martin (Bearb.), Salzburger Urkundenbuch, Bd. I, Traditionscodices, Salzburg 1910, Band II, Urkunden von 790–1199, Salzburg 1916.

Hellmuth, Acker und Wiesen = Thomas Hellmuth, „Acker und Wiesen wissen nichts von Patriotismus", in: Oskar Dohle, Thomas Mitterecker (Hg.), Salzburg im Ersten Weltkrieg. Fernab der Front – dennoch im Krieg (Schriftenreihe des Forschungsinstitutes für politische-historische Studien der Dr.-Wilfried-Haslauer-Bibliothek, Salzburg Band 48; Schriftenreihe des Archivs der Erzdiözese Salzburg 13; Schriftenreihe des Salzburger Landesarchivs Nr. 22), Wien-Köln-Weimar 2014, S. 47–59.

Hinterseer, Heimat-Chronik Lofer–St. Martin = Sebastian Hinterseer, Heimat-Chronik Lofer–St. Martin, Lofer o. J. (1982).

Hoffmann, Salzburg = Robert Hoffmann, Salzburg im Biedermeier. Die Stadt und ihre Einwohner in der ersten Hälfte des 19. Jahrhunderts, in: MGSL 120/121 (1980/1981), S. 219–274.

Höglinger, Die Stadtmauer im Sternbräu = Peter Höglinger, Die Stadtmauer im Sternbräu, in: Archäologie Österreichs 25/1 (2014), S. 32–36.

Hübner, Beschreibuang, 1. u. 2. Bd. = L(orenz) Hübner, Beschreibung der hochfürstlich- erzbischöflichen Haupt- und Residenzstadt Salzburg und ihrer Gegenden verbunden mit ihrer ältesten Geschichte, 1. Bd., Salzburg 1792, 2. Bd., Salzburg, 1793.

Mühlbacher, Die Residenz = Karin Mühlbacher, Die Residenz. Regierungs- und Wohnsitz des Landes- und Stadtherrn, in: Ammerer/Weidenholzer, Rathaus – Kirche – Wirt, S. 45–60.

Kaut, Salzburg von A–Z = Josef Kaut (Hg.), Salzburg von A–Z, Salzburg 1954.

Kernmayr, Brot und Eisen = Hans Gustl Kernmayr (Hg.), Brot und Eisen, Salzburg 1951.

Kerschbaumer, Faszination = Gert Kerschbaumer, Faszination Drittes Reich. Kunst und Alltag der Kulturmetropole Salzburg, Salzburg 1988.

Kerschbaumer, Gausuppe = Gert Kerschbaumer, Gausuppe und tausendjähriger Juchezer. Gasthauskultur im Dritten Reich – am Beispiel Salzburg, in: Zeitgeschichte, Heft 7, 11 (1983/1984), S. 213–234.

Klehr, Die Getreidegasse = Rudolph Klehr, Die Getreidegasse – mit Rathausplatz und Kranzlmarkt. Historische Erinnerungen bei Spaziergängen in der Salzburger Altstadt, Salzburg o. D. (1994).

Klein, Bevölkerung und Siedlung = Kurt Klein, Bevölkerung und Siedlung, in: Heinz Dopsch, Hans Spatzenegger (Hg.), Geschichte Salzburgs. Stadt und Land, II/2, Salzburg 1988, S. 1289–1360.

Kobes, K + K + K = Karl Kobes, K + K + K Salzburg, Kunst Küche Kur, Salzburg 1970.

Köfner, Geschichte Salzburgs = Gottfried Köfner, Geschichte Salzburgs in den Jahren 1918/1919 unter besonderer Berücksichtigung des Problems der Lebensmittelversorgung, phil. Diss., Salzburg 1979.

Kohl, Stockwerkseigentum = Gerald Kohl, Stockwerkseigentum – Geschichte, Theorie und Praxis der materiellen Gebäudeteilung unter besonderer Berücksichtigung von Rechtstatsachen aus Österreich (Schriften zur Europäischen Rechts- und Verfassungsgeschichte 55), Berlin 2007.

Kramml, Bruderhaus = Peter Kramml, Das Bruderhaus zu St. Sebastian. Vom spätmittelalterlichen Armenhaus und Hospital zum Versorgungs- und Altenheim des 19. Jahrhunderts, in: Thomas Weidenholzer, Erich Marx (Hg.), Hundert Jahre „Versorgungshaus Nonntal". Zur Geschichte der Alters- und Armenversorgung der Stadt Salzburg (Schriftenreihe des Archivs der Stadt Salzburg Nr. 9), Salzburg 1998, S. 111–160.

Kramml, Das Rathaus = Peter F. Kramml, Das Rathaus. Zentrales Bauwerk der Bürger, Symbol der Stadtobrigkeit und Sitz der Stadtverwaltung, in: Ammerer/ Weidenholzer, Rathaus – Kirche – Wirt, S. 11–33.

Kreibich, Salzburger Hofbrauereien = Heinz Kreibich, Die Geschichte der Salzburger Hofbrauereien 1498–1815, Diss., Innsbruck–Salzburg 1957.

Kunz, Monumentalbauten = Otto Kunz, Projektierte unausgeführte Monumentalbauten in Salzburg in den letzten sechzig Jahren, in: Salzburger Volksblatt 1.1.1930 (Jubiläumsausgabe), S. 17–24.

Lackner, Volksernährung = Josef Lackner, Die Volksernährung in Salzburg im 1. Weltkrieg. Hausarbeit aus Geschichte, Salzburg 1977.

Lichtblau, In Lebensgefahr = Albert Lichtblau, In Lebensgefahr: die jüdische Bevölkerung der Stadt Salzburg, in: Thomas Weidenholzer, ders. (Hg.), Leben im Terror. Verfolgung und Widerstand. Die Stadt Salzburg im Nationalsozialismus, Band 3 (Schriftenreihe des Archivs der Stadt Salzburg 35), Salzburg 2012, S. 64–109.

Lipburger, Das sogenannte Cristan Reutter'sche Stadtbuch = Michael Lipburger, Das sogenannte Cristan Reutter'sche Stadtbuch. Beiträge zur Geschichte der Stadt Salzburg zwischen dem Ratsbrief Friedrich III. von 1481 und der Stadt- und Polizeiordnung von 1524, Prüfungsarbeit am Institut für Österreichische Geschichtsforschung, Wien 1983.

Lipburger, Stadtrecht = Peter Michael Lipburger, Bürgerschaft und Stadtherr. Vom Stadtrecht des 14. Jahrhunderts zur Stadt- und Polizeiordnung des Kardinals Matthäus Lang (1524), in: Heinz Dopsch (Hg.), Vom Stadtrecht zur Bürgerbeteiligung. Festschrift 700 Jahre Stadtrecht von Salzburg (Salzburger Museum Carolino Augusteum Jahresschrift 33), Salzburg 1987, S. 40–63.

Lobenwein, Ordnungen und Mandate = Elisabeth Lobenwein, Die Ordnungen und Mandate des Marcus Sitticus, in: Gerhard Ammerer, Ingonda Hannesschläger, Peter Keller (Hg.), Erzbischof Marcus Sitticus von Hohenems 1612–1619. Kirche, Kunst und Hof in Salzburg zur Zeit der Gegenreformation. Beiträge der wissenschaftlichen Tagung in Salzburg. 15.–16. Juni 2012, Salzburg 2012, S. 103–110.

Marx, „Dann ging es Schlag auf Schlag" = Erich Marx, „Dann ging es Schlag auf Schlag". Die Bombenangriffe auf die Stadt Salzburg, in: Ders. (Hg.), Bomben auf Salzburg: die „Gauhauptstadt" im „Totalen Krieg" (Schriftenreihe des Archivs der Stadt Salzburg 6), Salzburg 1995, S. 139–274.

Mösenlechner, Firmengeschichte = Stefanie Mösenlechner, Die Firmengeschichte der Privatbrauerei M. C. Wieninger in Teisendorf, in: Salzfass. Heimatkundliche Zeitschrift des Historischen Vereins Rupertiwinkel e. V., Jg. Heft 1, 45 (2011), S. 62–84.

Mussoni, Eisengewerkschaft = Georg Mussoni, Die Eisengewerkschaft Achtal. Eine altsalzburgische Aktiengesellschaft. 1537–1919, in: MGSL 60 (1920), S. 1–32.

Neureiter/Zwink, Salzburg – wo? = Gerhard Neureiter, Eberhard Zwink, Salzburg – wo? Ein unentbehrlicher Führer durch die schöne Stadt Salzburg und ihre Umgebung mit Illustrationen und einem Stadtplan von Bettina Kemp, München 1969.

ÖKT XIII = Hans Tietze (Bearb.), Österreichische Kunsttopographie, Bd. XIII: Die profanen Denkmale der Stadt Salzburg, hg. v. Kunsthistorischen Institute der k. k. Zentralkommission für Denkmalpflege, Wien 1914.

Otruba, A. Hitler's „Tausend-Mark-Sperre" = Gustav Otruba, A. Hitler's „Tausend-Mark-Sperre" und die Folgen für Österreichs Fremdenverkehr (1933–1938) (Linzer Schriften zur Sozial- u. Wirtschaftsgeschichte 9), Linz 1983.

Pflanzl, Berta Pflanzl = Robert H. Pflanzl (Hg.), Berta Pflanzl. Vom Dienstmädchen zur gnädigen Frau, Wien 2009.

Preiß, Hofbrauhaus = Roswitha Preiß, Das ehemalige Hofbrauhaus in Henndorf, in: Alfred Stefan Weiß, Karl Ehrenfellner, Sabine Falk (Hg.), Henndorf am Wallersee, Kultur und Geschichte einer Salzburger Gemeinde, Henndorf 1992, S. 403–420.

Rau, Orte der Gastlichkeit = Susanne Rau, Orte der Gastlichkeit – Orte der Kommunikation. Aspekte der Raumkonstitution von Herbergen in der frühneuzeitlichen Stadt, in: Renate Dürr, Gerd Schwerhoff (Hg.), Kirchen Märkte und Tavernen. Erfahrungs- und Handlungsräume in der Frühen Neuzeit (Zeitsprünge. Forschungen zur Frühen Neuzeit), Frankfurt/Main 2005, S. 394–417.

Salzburg und Umgebung = Salzburg und Umgebung, Salzburg 1897.

Salzburg zur Zeit der Mozart = Katalog zur Ausstellung Salzburg zur Zeit der Mozart. Salzburger Museum CA – Die Bürgerstadt, 152. Sonderausstellung; Dommuseum zu Salzburg – Die Fürstenstadt, XV. Sonderausstellung, Salzburg 1991.

Salzburg, Stadt und Land = Salzburg, Stadt und Land, hg. vom Landesverband für Fremdenverkehr in Salzburg, Salzburg 1902.

Scheutz, Gaststätten = Martin Scheutz, „hab ichs auch im würthshauß da und dort gehört (…)". Gaststätten als multifunktionale öffentliche Orte im 18. Jahrhundert, in: Ders., Wolfgang Schmale, Dana Štefanová (Hg.), Orte des Wissens (Jahrbuch der Österreichischen Gesellschaft zur Erforschung des achtzehnten Jahrhunderts 18/19), Bochum 2004, S. 169–203.

Schobersberger, Baumeister = Walburga Schobersberger, Baumeister einer Epoche. Das gründerzeitliche Wirken der Baumeister- und Architektenfamilie Ceconi in Stadt und Land Salzburg, in: MGSL 125 (1985), S. 703–729.

Schwarz, Besucher Salzburgs = Heinrich Schwarz, Besucher Salzburgs. Künstler, Musiker, Dichter, Gelehrte und Staatsmänner. Auszüge aus den Fremdenanzeigen 1815–1830, in: MGSL 100 (1960), S. 487–527.

Spatzenegger, Blaue Gans = Hans Spatzenegger, Gasthaus zur „Blauen Gans". Fürstenbier, Bürgermeister, Mozart-Freunde, Salzburg o. D. (2006).

Spechtler/Uminsky, Stadt- und Polizeiordnung = Franz Viktor Spechtler, Rudolf Uminsky (Hg.), Die Salzburger Stadt- und Polizeiordnung von 1524. Rechtshistorische Einleitung von Peter Putzer (Göppinger Arbeiten zur Germanistik Nr. 222), Göppingen 1978.

Sternbräu Salzburg = Sternbräu Salzburg. Zur Salvator-Probe am 16. März 1899, Salzburg o. J. (1899).

Sungler, Bürgerstuben = Adele Sungler, Bürgerstuben, Bürgerhäuser, Bürgerstolz: Karl Reisenbichler, ein Salzburger Maler, in: Bastei, Heft 1, 55 (2006), S. 26–30.

Süß, Bürgermeister = Vinzenz Maria Süß, Die Bürgermeister in Salzburg von 1433–1840. Mit den Bildnissen derselben aus den noch jetzt in Salzburg lebenden Familien und des berühmten Sigmund Hafner Edlen von Imbachshausen, Salzburg 1940.

Wagner, Die erste Barockisierung = Franz Wagner, Die erste Barockisierung der Stiftskirche St. Peter und die Altäre des Hans Waldburger, in: Festschrift St. Peter zu Salzburg 582–1982 (Studien und Mitteilungen zur Geschichte des Benediktiner-Ordens und seiner Zweige, hg. von der bayerischen Benediktinerakademie. Der ganzen Reihe 93, Jg. 1982, Heft I–II), St. Ottilien 1982, S. 627–652.

Waitzbauer/Wagner, 500 Jahre = Harald Waitzbauer, Christoph Wagner, 500 Jahre Salzburger Stiegl-Bier 1492–1992, Wien 1992.

Wallentin, Santino Solari = Ingeborg Wallentin, Der Salzburger Hofbaumeister Santino Solari (1576–1646). Leben und Werk auf Grund der historischen Quellen, Diss., Salzburg 1985.

Weidenholzer, Das „Höllbräu" = Thomas Weidenholzer, Das „Höllbräu" – Zur Geschichte eines Salzburger Braugasthofes von 1700 bis in die Gegenwart, in: Erich Marx (Hg.), Das „Höllbräu" zu Salzburg. Geschichte eines Braugasthofes (Schriftenreihe des Archivs der Stadt Salzburg 4), Salzburg 1992, S. 61–132.

Weidenholzer, Not = Thomas Weidenholzer, Not und Luxus, Korruption, Antisemitismus und Radikalisierung, in: Oskar Dohle, Thomas Mitterecker (Hg.), Salzburg im Ersten Weltkrieg. Fernab der Front – dennoch im Krieg (Schriftenreihe des Forschungsinstitutes für politisch-historische Studien der Dr.-Wilfried-Haslauer-Bibliothek, Salzburg Band 48; Schriftenreihe des Archivs der Erzdiözese Salzburg 13; Schriftenreihe des Salzburger Landesarchivs Nr. 22), Wien-Köln-Weimar 2014, S. 61–89.

Weidenholzer, Zum Stern = Thomas Weidenholzer, Zum Stern, in: Ammerer/Angermüller, Das Salzburger Mozart-Lexikon, S. 546 f.

Weilmeyr, Salzburg = Franz Xaver Weilmeyr, Salzburg, die Hauptstadt des Salzach-Kreises, Ein Hand- und Adreß-Buch für Jedermann, Salzburg 1813.

Zauner, Auszug Landesgesetze = Judas Thaddäus Zauner, Auszug der wichtigsten hochfürstl. Salzburgischen Landesgesetze zum gemeinnützigen Gebrauch nach alphabetischer Ordnung, Bd. 1–3, Salzburg 1785–1790.

Zillner, Geschichte I = F. V. Zillner, Geschichte der Stadt Salzburg. I. Buch. Geschichtliche Stadtbeschreibung, Salzburg 1885.

Zillner, Geschichte II = F.V. Zillner, Geschichte der Stadt Salzburg. II. Buch. Zeitgeschichte bis zum Ausgange des 18. Jahrhunderts, Salzburg 1890.

Dr. Harald Waitzbauer

Research associate at the Salzburg Open-Air Museum, writer, publications on the history of Salzburg, including *500 Jahre Salzburger Stiegl-Bier 1492–1992* (1992), *375 Jahre Augustiner Brau Kloster Mulln in Salzburg* (1996), *Zum Wilden Mann. Geschichte eines Salzburger Gasthauses* (2009).

Prof. Gerhard Ammerer

Deputy head of the Department of History at Salzburg University, publications on Habsburg and Salzburg history, including *Das Salzburger Mozart-Lexikon* (with Rudolph Angermuller, 2005), *Das Tomaselli und die Salzburger Kaffeehauskultur seit 1700* (2006), *Die Getreidegasse* (with Jutta Baumgartner, 2011).

Gerhard Ammerer, Harald Waitzbauer

WIRTSHÄUSER
Eine Kulturgeschichte der Salzburger Gaststätten

224 Seiten, 24,5 x 30,5 cm
durchgehend farbig und s/w bebildert
Hardcover
€ 35,00
ISBN 978-3-7025-0750-3

www.pustet.at